A

Anger Management

Swati Y. Bhave
Sunil Saini

SAGE www.sagepublications.com
Los Angeles • London • New Delhi • Singapore • Washington DC

First published in 2009 by

SAGE Publications India Pvt Ltd
B1/I-1 Mohan Cooperative Industrial Area
Mathura Road, New Delhi 110 044, India
www.sagepub.in

SAGE Publications Inc
2455 Teller Road
Thousand Oaks, California 91320, USA

SAGE Publications Ltd
1 Oliver's Yard, 55 City Road
London EC1Y 1SP, United Kingdom

SAGE Publications Asia-Pacific Pte Ltd
33 Pekin Street
#02-01 Far East Square
Singapore 048763

Published by Vivek Mehra for SAGE Publications India Pvt Ltd, typeset in 10/13 pt AGaramond by Star Compugraphics Private Limited, Delhi and printed at Chaman Enterprises, New Delhi.

Library of Congress Cataloging-in-Publication Data

Bhave, Swati Y.
    Anger management/authored by Swati Y. Bhave and Sunil Saini.
        p. cm.
    Includes bibliographical references and index.
    1. Anger   I. Saini, Sunil.   II. Title.

BF575.A5B49   152.4'7—dc22   2009   2009022978

ISBN: 978-81-321-0085-0 (PB)

The SAGE Team: Reema Singhal, Sejuti Dasgupta, Vijay Sah and Trinankur Banerjee

I dedicate this book to my husband Yashwant Bhave . . . living with him for last 35 years I learnt from his day to day behavior that it is possible to control your anger even under grave provocation. Living with a person who does not get angry gives a lot of peace and happiness. Over the years I have also managed to harness my anger to a great extent and hence was motivated to write this book

Swati Y. Bhave

The book is dedicated to my parents

Sunil Saini

Contents

SECTION TWO

Various Effects of Anger on People

SECTION THREE

Dealing with Anger

Preface

Anger is an emotional response when we face an obstruction in reaching our target. Everyday life is filled with many such examples when we do not get what we desire and get frustrated and angry. The anger management book is written to help laymen to understand these everyday conflicting situations leading to anger and related problems, and how to manage these effectively. Psychologists, psychiatrists, and other health specialists are working on many psychological problems like stress, depression, aggression, and other conduct problems. Despite all this, there is still a lack of work on anger management for the layman. The present book is concerned with how anger develops in everyday life situation of laymen, and how they experience, express anger, and develop health problems.

Many books have been written on anger and related problems in different parts of the world. No single book is perfect. There is no good book on anger management for the layman especially in India. In the present book, we have tried our best to make it reader-friendly for every layman to reconstruct their negative thoughts, feelings, and behaviors to mange their everyday anger problem, so that we can have a better home, school or workplace, and mental peace at an individual level can be created for the betterment of society and world peace.

We often see that most of the everyday conflicts like parent-child aggression, marital discard, poor school performance, school bullying, teacher–child violence, frustration due to workload, unachievable targets, and personal problems like stress, depression, aggression, road rage, are rooted in one common problem 'Anger'. Therefore, a layman is confounded with anger coming from different sources. Keeping this in mind, we planned to write this book.

The first section of the book examines how anger develops in everyday life, how we experience it, express or suppress it, and control it. The most important feature of our book is that all these have been explained with illustrations which would help a layman to understand how anger develops in everyday life and how to manage it. This section also contains important information regarding anger assessment tools.

The second section of the book discusses the effects of anger, how long it lasts, why does it occur, what happens to your body when anger occurs, and how does it progress in physiological problems (like hypertension, stroke, lung disease, diabetes, cancer, arthritis, obesity, and physical pain), psychological problems (like depression, stress, eating disorders, body dissatisfaction, and suicidal ideation), and behavioral problems (like aggression, dating violence, marital conflict, road rage, alcohol and drug abuse, sensation seeking, and impulsivity). Researches have shown that anger and its associates, hostility and aggression, collectively called the AHA-Syndrome have been related with increased risk of cardiovascular diseases. We have written a book intitled *AHA Syndrome and Cardiovascular Disease*, which will be published in August 2009.

The third section of the book is focused on anger management tips for the self, and at family, school, and workplace. These A to Z tips for anger management are also expressed with line cartoons. These are so simple and illustrative that if one would go through these tips, he/she would surely have anger reduced. At a clinical level, we have provided some very important and effective therapies to deal with chronic anger.

An appendix has been provided to list the various definitions of anger starting from Plato, Aristotle to the present researchers like Spielberger, Novaco, and Deffenbacher. The appendix aims at helping the layman understand better the concept of anger and how different researchers have defined it.

We hope that after having read this book every layman would decide to keep it as a permanent part of his library or collection of books.

Acknowledgements

We would like to acknowledge the important contribution of Dr Manoj Chhabra, a national level cartoonist, who has drawn excellent cartoons based on our specifications, which have made this book more interesting to read.

We thank Dr Sugata Ghosh, Leela Kirloskar, and Reema Singhal of SAGE Publications for accepting the manuscript with great interest.

Swati Y. Bhave

I am very grateful to Dr Swati Bhave for having faith, and encouragement in our second joint effort and for making all the figures apart from the cartoons for this book. I am especially thankful to Mr Mukesh Kumar, Incharge, UCIC, and his staff members at GJUS&T, Hisar, for their continuous support for all things. Finally, special thanks go to Neelam Goyal who helped me a lot in my other assignments simultaneously.

Sunil Saini

Key Concepts and Terms

Addiction

Addiction is the compulsive need to use a habit-forming substance, or an irresistible urge to engage in a behavior.

Adolescence

The period of transition from childhood to adulthood (the WHO definition is from 10–19 years of age.)

Aggression

Aggression is the intentional harming of others physically, psychologically, and socially.

AHA-Syndrome

The triad of anger, hostility, and aggression.

Annoyance

Annoyance is an unpleasant mental state that is characterized by such effects as irritation and distraction from one's conscious thinking and leads to anger.

Anorexia nervosa

Anorexia nervosa is a condition characterized by an inadequate and unhealthy pattern of eating and excessive concern with the control of body weight and shape.

Anxiety

A state of apprehension, tension, and worry.

Behavior therapy

A method of psychotherapy based on learning principles.

Body dissatisfaction

Body dissatisfaction is negative evaluation of one's figure and body parts.

Bulimia nervosa

Bulimia nervosa is a condition of eating disorder characterized by overeating and then purging to get rid of the calories consumed.

Child abuse

Intentional actions that result in harm to a child's physical or psychological well-being.

Cognitive behavior therapy	A therapy that attempts to help people identify the kind of stressful situations that produce their physiological or emotional symptoms and alter the way they cope with these situation.
Cognitive restructuring	A cognitive behavior modification procedure in which the client learns to identify thoughts that are distressing and then learns to get rid of those thoughts or to replace them with more desirable thoughts.
Compassion	Compassion is an understanding of the emotional state of another or oneself.
Corporal punishment	Corporal punishment is the deliberate infliction of pain and suffering intended to change a person's behavior or to punish them.
Depression	Depression is a mood disorder characterized by intense feelings of loss, sadness, hopelessness, failure, and rejection. The two major types of mood disorder are unipolar disorder, also called major depression, and bipolar disorder, whose sufferers are termed manic-depressive.
Disappointment	Disappointment is the feeling of dissatisfaction that follows the failure of expectations to manifest.
Displacement	The redirection of feelings toward an object, person or situation that is less threatening than the actual source of the feelings.
Eating disorder	Severe disturbance in eating behavior characterized by preoccupation with weight and unhealthy efforts to control weight.
Empathy	Empathy is the ability to understand the situation of others.
Emotion	Powerful, largely uncontrollable feelings accompanied by physiological changes.
Emotional intelligence	Emotional intelligence (EI) is defined as an ability, capacity, or skill to perceive, assess, and manage the emotions of one's self, of others, and of groups.

Fear	Fear is an intense aversion to or apprehension of a person, place, activity, event, or object that causes emotional distress and often avoidance behavior.
Frustration	The feeling that occurs in any situation in which our goal is thwarted.
Frustration tolerance	Frustration tolerance is the ability of a person on a task when frustration occurs due to setbacks and difficulty.
Hostility	Hostility is an attitude that involves disliking others and evaluating them negatively.
Humor	Humor is the ability of people, objects, situations or words to evoke feelings of amusement or happiness in people. A sense of humor is the ability to experience humor.
Hypnosis	Hypnosis is a dream like state that resembles sleep but is induced by a person whose suggestions are readily accepted by the subject.
Impulsivity	Impulsivity is the failure to resist an impulse, drive, or temptation to perform an act that is harmful to others.
Intelligence quotient	An intelligence quotient or IQ is a score derived from one of the several different standardized tests attempting to measure intelligence.
Jealousy	Jealousy typically refers to the thoughts, feelings, and behaviors that occur when a person believes a valued relationship is being threatened by a rival.
Learning disability	Learning disability is a group of disorders manifested by significant differences in the acquisition and use of listening, speaking, reading, writing, reasoning, or mathematical skill.
Migraine	Headache characterized by recurrent attacks of severe pain, usually on one side of the head. It may be preceded by flashes or spots before the eyes or ringing in the ears, and

	accompanied by double vision, nausea, vomiting, or dizziness.
Mindfulness	Mindfulness is a skill which enables to pay attention to the present moment in a non-judgmental way.
Obesity	Obesity is the condition characterized by increased body weight due to excessive accumulation of fat.
Optimism	Optimism is an outlook on life such that one maintains a view of the world as a positive place.
Peer pressure	Peer pressure is the influence of a social group (same age group friends) on an individual.
Personality	The distinctive and characteristic pattern of thoughts, emotions and behavior that define an individual's personal style of interacting with others.
Pessimism	Pessimism is the decision to evaluate something as negative when 't is uncommon to do so.
Prejudice	Prejudice is the premature judgment or positive/negative attitude toward a person or group of people which is not based on objective facts.
Rational-emotive therapy	An approach that focuses on altering client's pattern of irrational thinking to reduce maladaptive emotions and behavior.
Road rage	Road rage is a term used to refer to violent behavior by a driver of an automobile, which thus causes accidents or incidents on roadways. It can be thought of as an extreme case of aggressive driving.
Resentment	Unresolved anger over a negative event which occurred in the past.
Revenge	Revenge consists primarily of retaliation against a person or group in response to a perceived wrongdoing.

Self-efficacy	Self-efficacy is one's belief about one's ability to perform behavior that should lead to expected outcome.
Sensation seeking	Sensation seeking is characterized as the need for varied, novel, complex, and intense sensations and experiences, and the willingness to take physical, social, legal, and financial risks for the sake of such experiences.
State anger	State anger is situation specific and is defined as a psychobiological emotional state or condition marked by subjective feelings that vary in intensity from mild irritation or annoyance to intense fury and rage.
Stress	Experiencing an event that is perceived as endangering one's physical or psychological well-being.
Stroke	A stroke, also called a cerebral vascular accident (CVA), is the sudden death of cells in a specific area of the brain due to inadequate blood flow.
Suicidal ideation	Suicidal ideation is a common medical term for thoughts about suicide, which may be as detailed as a formulated plan, without the suicidal act itself.
Systematic desensitization	A behavior therapy used to reduce clients anxiety responses through counterbalancing.
Tantrum	A tantrum is an emotional outburst wherein the higher brain functions are unable to stop the emotional expression of the lower (emotional and physical) brain functions. It can be categorized by an irrational fit of crying, screaming, defiance, and a resistance to every attempt at pacification in which even physical control is lost.
Temperament	Temperament is a typical style of behavior such as emotional, intense, persistence, introvert, extrovert, impulsive, slow and fast.

Therapy	Therapy is the attempted remediation of a health problem, usually following a diagnosis.
Trait anger	Trait anger is the stable personality trait and defined as individual difference in the disposition to perceive a wide range of situations as annoying or frustrating.

SECTION ONE

Anger: Causes, Expressions, and Types

INTRODUCTION

In the chaotic world of today, day to day life situations are filled with a lot of negative emotions leading to anger, stress, and depression. Fear, insecurity, threats, disappointments, and frustrations are common problems in almost every society, which generate a lot of anger in the human mind.

Emotions are very complex in their origin and in their effects. Emotions appear early in life and have significant impact on emotional reactions. Each emotion has an inherently adaptive function, but growing children must learn to regulate and modify their emotion expression, so that they do not become maladaptive (Izard, 1993). Emotions and emotional styles are the building blocks of a person's unique, relatively stable, and consistent pattern of personality, which dispose him or her to feel, think, and behave in a particular way (Spielberger et al., 1995).

Anger, the most often expressed human emotion, expressed several times a day by any individual (Avrill, 1983) can be the consequence of many internal and external factors (Novaco, 2000) including biological, psychological, behavioral, and social. All these have to be defined in family, peer, media, and social contexts.

Internal factors include the type of personality, lack of problem solving skills, unpleasant memories, effects of hormones, anxiety, depression, hostility, tension, agitation, problems of the nervous system, etc. The presence of a prior negative affect state may intensify anger and lower the ability to control self (Berkowitz and Harmonjones, 2004).

External factors include negative parental practices, situational and environmental factors (traffic jams, barking dogs, horn honking, loud noise, etc.), effect of peers and media, socio-economic status, social stress, etc.

In today's fast growing, competitive, and technologically advanced life, positive emotions have lost their meanings. Terrorist activities around the world have threatened humanity and made everyone feel insecure all the time. Many negative emotions especially insecurity and fear can be transformed into the emotion of Anger.

Hence people at every developmental stage, from a small child to an old person, are in the grip of the deadliest emotion that is Anger.

Figure 1.1   Angry people

Father scolding a child   A man throwing a temper tantrum

A woman angry with her computer

Anger among school children is increasing day by day. Students are known to carry weapons in their school bags; massacres using guns are being reported in schools around the world. It is unfortunate that gun shot killings of peers by teenage boys was reported in our country also last year. Girls are reported to be as angry as boys. They are more likely than boys to kick, push, bite, slap, and hit in anger, especially when they are jealous (Trama and Saini, 2009).

In youths, emotional problems and marital disappointments are increasing, leading to a number of negative emotions. Unfortunately, youth often indulge in aggression, and commit serious crimes like robbery, driving accidents, drug abuse, dating violence, and date rape. Sensation seeking and other impulse control behaviors are also on rise, which have strong relation with anger and aggression (Joireman, Anderson, and Strathman, 2003).

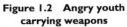

Figure 1.2 Angry youth carrying weapons

Anger management therefore is crucial at every stage of life.

An attempt has been made in the present book to provide some best practices on anger management for parents, teachers, and laypersons in the community.

It is very interesting to read the different definitions of anger by various philosophers and psychologists (see Appendix).

ANGER EXPERIENCE

WHEN DOES ANGER OCCUR?

Desire, the root of our anger, arises only when there is an awareness of one's being, i.e., of 'I am'. This awareness is pleasurable and a human being feels desire for repetition of this pleasure in various ways. When frustrated, human desires cause distress because these desires have selfish motives and are fulfilled at the cost of others' discomfort or sufferings (Ramsukhdas, 1996).

According to Hindu mythology, *satwa* (goodness, knowledge XIV-6) *rajas* (activity, passion XIV-7), and *tamas* (ignorance, inactivity XIV-8) are the three *gunas*, which determine one's personality and behavior. People dominated by *rajas* are 'given to lust and anger and they strive to obtain, by unlawful means, hoards of wealth for sensual enjoyments' (XVI-12 Chinmayananda trans., 1976; Ram, 2009).

Everyone has had angry feelings at some time or other. It is a normal reaction when circumstances are not fair or our expectations are not met. Anger over these unmet expectations often lead us to blame others and be aggressive toward them. Hence *'Other blame'* that is, an assessment by the individual that someone or something has wrongly caused the negative situation to occur, is highly associated with anger (Avrill, 1983; Kassinove, 1995). The perception of another's blameworthiness always leads to anger (Crick and Dodge, 1994).

Anger is an emotional state that can be caused by both internal and external sources. Anger can be elicited by behaviors of self or others or specific events, and a combination of internal and external events.

- When we do not get what we want, at a particular moment, i.e., internal source, a flash of anger overwhelms us (Avrill, 1982).
- This also can happen when we do not get the recognition or acceptance that we think we deserve (Kemper, 1987).
- Anger is likely to occur when a person believes that his personal rights or codes have been violated.
- Anger is also likely when an individual perceives a threat against self-esteem (Lazarus, 1991).
- Anger may be a response to the action of an environmental stressor (e.g., traffic jam).
- Emotions like frustration, anger, and rage occur as a result of the omission of a positive reinforcer or the termination of a positive reinforcer (Mowrer, 1960).
- Appraisal theorists argue that anger is evoked in negatively apprised situations. These situations are described as situations where the individual's goals are blocked (Roseman et al., 1990). The appraisal of unfairness (Ellsworth and Smith, 1988) and others accountability are considered as core components of anger (Ellsworth, 1994).
- Lewis (1993) proposed that the thwarting of a goal-directed action is an unlearned cause of anger.
- Anger and aggression are also mediated by cognitive variables, such as attitudes, beliefs, attributions, motives, and faulty information processing. These factors can include hostile attribution bias (i.e., one sees hostility where none exists), quick judgment, omission of important cues, and incorrect prediction of outcomes (Dodge and Petit, 2003).
- People become angry when they perceive or believe that they may lose resources that they deserve or to which they are entitled to (DiGiuseppe and Tafrate, 2006).
- Anger results from the perception of an injustice, lack of fairness, or grievance (Tedeschi and Nesler, 1993).

Any unpleasant situation like pain, discomfort, frustration, or social stress provokes a negative affect. This negative affect is associated with fight and flight motivation (Berkowitz, 1983).

Figure 1.3   Model for a fight and flight situation

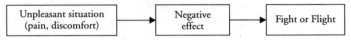

An individual's prior experiences form associations that provide cues relating to the present situation. If these cues lead him or her to desire primarily to escape then the 'flight system' is activated and the person experience mostly fear. If the cues lead him or her to a desire *to attack,* then the *fight system* is activated and he or she experiences mostly anger (Dollard et al., 1939).

Both expression and suppression of anger are useful under different circumstances. In some situations, anger inhibition is most useful and in others anger expression is helpful.

Anger inhibition

Inhibition of anger is valuable to change bad habits, to reduce our attention to unwanted thoughts and behaviors, or to deal with circumstances that are beyond our control. When anger is inhibited, the individual has not directly dealt with the anger stimulus and consequently may relive the experience for some time (Harburg et al., 2003). In adults, inhibiting anger has been linked with elevated blood pressure (Helmers et al., 2000).

Anger expression

Expression of anger or grief can decrease one's well-being (Bushman, 2002). However, researchers are of the view that neither expression nor inhibition of anger makes us better or worse.

'Anger is the emotion that is best recognized in social interaction.' In a marital conflict study, 79 percent of the wives experienced conflict and the expression of anger was good and helpful with regard to their relationships (Jenkins, Smith, and Graham, 1989).

It is seen that men more frequently perpetrate violence on women than vice versa. This could be intimately tied up with a man feeling that he is privileged and entitled to treat the women's body as *his* possession, which he is free to attack (Goldner et al., 1990).

NEGATIVE EXPERIENCES WITH THE ATTACHMENT FIGURE (e.g., siblings, parents, grandparents)

Most anger episodes occur between people who are close to each other. In 63 percent of the cases, anger was expressed to demonstrate authority and independence, thereby restoring the image of the self as strong (Averill, 1982).

Structural family therapy throws light on anger expression on the basis of nature of family organizations in constructing experiences. Key concepts include the ideas of boundary, hierarchy, and sub-systems in families (Procter and Dallos, 2006).

- A child in a sibling hierarchy may be furious because his younger brother has sat down next to his father.
- A son feels a sense of intrusion into his personal space when his mother comes to tidy his bedroom.
- A father becomes angry because his son does not offer him the respect that he feels is his due.

WHAT DOES ANGER DO TO US?

When anger occurs, the body goes instantly into a series of mind–body reactions that involves hormones, the nervous system, and the muscles. There is a release of adrenaline, which results in shortness of breath, skin flushing, muscle rigidity, and tightening of the jaw, stomach, shoulder, and hands that mobilize the body for an immediate anger reaction (Novaco, 2000). Anger exhausts a person after this reaction is over.

Figure 1.4   Effects of anger

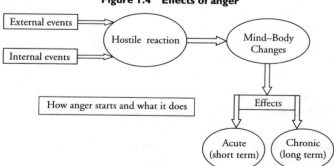

Is Anger a Good Emotion?

- Anger is a normal reaction and encountered in almost everyday life situations, e.g., at home, school, in public place, workplace, interpersonal relationships, etc.
- It is a healthy human emotion. In its healthy form, anger provides a warning signal to the brain that something is wrong and supplies the body with energy in the form of adrenaline to correct the situation.
- The unique adaptive function of anger is mobilization of energy to take action (Thomas, 2002).
- The way we express our anger can either be harmful or healthy.

Positive Aspects of Anger

We need anger for our survival. Anger helps a person to cope with a wide variety of situations. When anger is expressed in a constructive, non-hostile manner, it may have positive outcomes, such as expressing important feelings, identifying problems, redressing concerns, and motivating effective behavior (Averill, 1982; Novaco, 1975). Constructive use of anger is associated with lower blood pressure and better health (Davidson et al., 2000).

- When we allow ourselves to experience anger, it focuses our minds and strengthens our resolve. The experience of anger also results in increased social status (Tiedens, 2001), ameliorated interpersonal relationships (Averill, 1983), and justice behavior (Leach, Iyer, and Pedersen, 2006).
- If we did not have anger we would not be able to assert ourselves in the world. Many studies have investigated coping in the context of anger (Herrald and Tomaka, 2002) and Deffenbacher et al. (2001) also found a positive relationship between emotional intensity and action tendencies or behaviors.
- Anger can give us energy and motivation to right a wrong and to solve a problem; the same anger can be destructive if it is not expressed appropriately.
- Anger can be an effective release of tension, and can be a cue to correct wrongs. When used effectively, anger can get results and thus, it can force you to grow, adapt, and change (Eastman and Rozen, 1994).

- An athlete uses this energy to gain the power and momentum to win the game.
- History shows, anger gave the main thrust to social and civil revolutions. Therefore, anger can be a good motivator for creating a change.

Box 1.1   Positive aspects of anger

- Anger is a normal reaction.
- Positive way of expressing anger is a healthy emotion.
- Anger provides warning signal to the brain and gives body and mind with energy in the form of adrenaline to correct the situation.
  - An athlete uses this energy to gain the power and momentum to win the game.
  - Good motivator for creating social changes.
- It is ok to be angry but no ok to be mean.

How is Anger Expressed Negatively?

- Constantly repeating similar actions and words in certain situations.
- Frequent swearing, use of violent language and behavior.
- Brooding over anger and fantasizing about negative situations.
- Not solving a problem, just getting angry about the situation.
- Having strong prejudice about others because of caste, creed, race, gender, age, etc.
- Constantly blaming others for fault.
- Getting violent in almost every social interaction, e.g., with school teachers, police, and public at bus stop, railway station, bank, shopkeepers, and administration.

What Happens When Anger is Expressed in a Negative Way?

Anger becomes negative when people deny it, suppress it, or express it inappropriately. Anger suppression correlates positively with pain assessment and intensity, pain behaviors, and interference with daily functioning and negatively with pain tolerance (Gelkopf, 1997; Kerns, Rosenberg, and Jacob, 1994).

- Negatively expressed anger may lead to negative evaluations by others, a negative self-concept and low self-esteem, family conflict, abusive parenting patterns, school bullying, and mild to severe aggression (Kassinove, 1995; Deffenbecher, Oetting and DiGiuseppe, 2002).
- Negative expression of anger can be physical in the form of assault, aggression, attack, and verbal in the form of hatred, criticism, contempt, suspicion, argument, resentment, irritation, jealous, envy, and name-calling (Avrill, 1982; Frijda, Kuipers and Ster chure, 1989).
- The other negative expressions include crying, teasing, yelling, sarcasm, attack, violence, crime, rape, murder, traffic accidents, child abuse, marital conflicts, divorce, troubled relationships, job loss, and financial risks (Novaco, 1986; Anderson, 2000).
- Anger is not necessarily involved in violent crime but works as dispositional risk factor for violence (Howells and Day, 2002; Novaco, Ramm, and Black, 2001).

Box 1.2   Negative aspects of anger

- Uncontrolled anger leads to 'negative emotions'
   • Hostility, resentment, bitterness, and hate
   • Destructive aggression
- Verbal aggression
   • Criticism, contempt, suspicion, argument, irritation, jealousy, envy, and name-calling.
- Physical aggression
   • Assault, molestation, and murder
   • Sports and driving aggression
   • Domestic violence and rape

An acute episode of anger can precipitate a heart attack or brain stroke and even lead to death (Suinn, 2001).

CHRONIC ANGER LEADS TO HOSTILITY AND AGGRESSION

- Such a state of mind makes a person indulge in acts of violence and revenge, which he later regrets.
- Chronic anger affects all the body organs leading to various diseases like attention-deficient hyperactivity disorders (ADHD) and

obsessive–compulsive disorder (Bannon, Gonsalvbez, Craft, and Boyce, 2002; Barkley, 1997).

- Negative health consequences of chronic anger are more smoking, frequent drinking, suicidal actions, headaches, hypertension, ulcers, heart diseases, stroke, and diabetes.
- Chronic anger can lead to emotional problems like anxiety, depression, poor concentration, lack of confidence, helplessness, and mood swings (Deffenbacher, 1992; Deffenbacher et al., 1996). Morris et al. (1981) found that anger was the only attribute, which successfully distinguished between benign and malignant breast disease. They further demonstrated that both extreme suppressors and extreme expressers of anger had higher rates of diagnosed breast cancer than women with moderate or normal emotional behavior. Similarly, less anger suppression was found to be associated with greater natural killer cell cytotoxicity (NKCC) in patients of prostate cancer (Penedo et al., 2006).

Excessive anger often turns into hostile attitude that sets people against each other, or even against themselves.

- If anger is expressed inappropriately, it can turn into other disturbing emotions such as hostility, resentment, bitterness, hatred, and other health problems (Deffenbacher et al., 2002).
- Uncontrolled anger transforms into destructive aggression having impact on personal well-being, families, work setting, and society.
- Anger causes high levels of arousal and energy that can last for hours or even longer. This persistent behavior results in aggression. The anger and subsequent aggression outburst may develop into an additive process of need satisfaction in serial killers (Tsytsarev and Grodnitzky, 1995).
- Anger can also be expressed in the forms of many anti-social behaviors.
- Emotionally, it may include responses like feelings of mild displeasure, fury, or rage.
- Research shows that angered and distressed individuals can direct aggression at persons who have not caused the distress (Berkowitz, 1993).
- Expression of anger while driving is a common phenomenon nowadays. Day by day, increase in road clashes, traffic accidents, and deaths, are the results of negative thoughts while driving. Research has also shown that in driving simulations, high anger drivers were twice as

likely to become involved in a motor vehicle accident, when under a high stress situations (Deffenbacher et al., 2003).

WHEN DOES ANGER BECOME PROBLEMATIC?

Anger can be both positive and negative according to its way of expression. The most important thing is to simply learn how to express our anger in appropriate, conscious, supportive ways. Anger becomes problematic when it lasts for a prolonged period. Prolongation of anger is a substantial factor in essential hypertension (Johnson, 1990).

When anger does not return to baseline, there are likely to be 'excitation transfer' effects, whereby the undissipated arousal adds to arousal activation from new sources and raise the probability of aggression (Zillman and Bryant, 1974).

Figure 1.5 Anger expression makes it easy to get an umpire's decision in sports (e.g., in cricket)

Figure 1.6 Forgive your partner otherwise you would regret it later

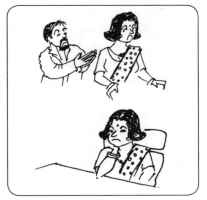

How a person expresses anger in a given situation depends on his past experiences, values, and beliefs. Individuals learn what are the socially or culturally appropriate responses to express anger, from the various experiences in their lives, from their families, friends, and community. Problematic anger has been implicated in the etiology of many psychosomatic symptoms (Piko, Keresztes, and Pluhar, 2006).

Murphy and Oberlin (2001) stress, '*It is sometimes okay to be angry, but it's never okay to be mean. Every angry reaction to a difficult situation has a line that separates the acceptable from the unacceptable.*' It is not the event that causes us to feel angry, but it is how we view the event and provocations that cause us to respond in a specific way (Luhn, 1992).

Anger can be used to justify oppressing others, to elevate our low self-worth, to hide other feelings, and to displace other emotions, such as using aggression to hide fear.

ANGER EXPRESSION

Anger is expressed in three ways. *It can be directed outward against others, directed inward leading to self-destructive behaviors and can be controlled* (Spielberger, 1999).

1. Destructive expressions of anger are when a person expresses it by yelling, screaming, punching someone, smashing or destroying something, or throwing a chair or book across the room.
2. Anger can be directed inward or be suppressed. This mode of expression can also be destructive unless anger is allowed to take some form of constructive external expression. It can increase the risks of high blood pressure, depression, suicide, gastrointestinal problems, respiratory diseases and can lead to more smoking and drinking, reckless and dangerous behavior, or failure at school, etc.
3. The best way to express anger is the positive way of anger expression or the control of anger or anger management. Controlling of anger involves calming oneself so that it can be used constructively.

Figure 1.7 Expression of anger

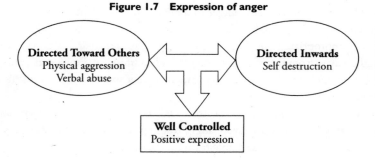

Thus, we can say that anger affects us negatively at all four levels of our beting—the physical, emotional, mental, and spirtitual levels.

Figure 1.8   Negative effects of anger

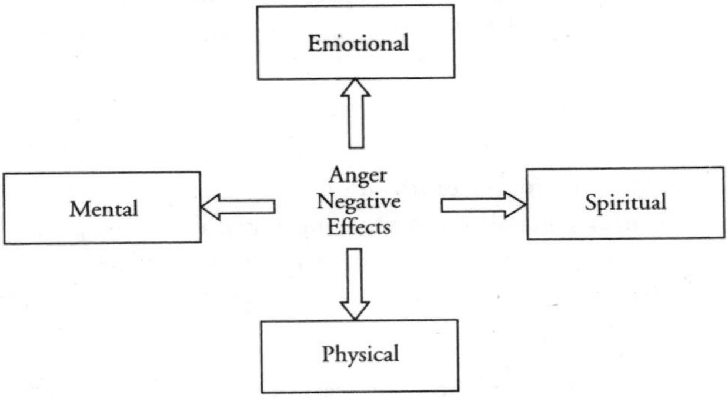

ANGER AT THE FAMILY LEVEL

In angry families, 'children progress steadily from learning to be disobedient to learning to be physically assaultive' (Tavris, 1989: 307). It starts with a three-step process that happens almost everyday.

- First, the child is attacked, criticized, or yelled at by an exasperated adult or sibling.
- Then the child responds aggressively.
- By doing this, the third step comes into play and this is where the aggression is rewarded by the attacker withdrawing. Through this process, the child is learning manipulative and coercive tactics as a substitute for social skills (Tavris, 1989).

MEASUREMENTS OF ANGER EXPRESSION

There are several useful scales that differentiate modes of anger expression.

1. **State-Trait Anger Expression Inventory (STAXI-2) by Spielberger (1999)**

Spielberger's (1999) State-Trait Anger Expression Inventory (STAXI-2) distinguishes among state-anger, trait-anger, anger-out, anger-in, anger-control/out, and anger-control/in.

a. State-anger: situation is specific and not stable.

b. Trait-anger: stable personality trait that leads to angry reactions.

c. Anger-in: anger withheld and suppressed. This is a characteristic of individuals who have anxiety and depression.

d. Anger-out: anger expressed openly physically, verbally, or toward the source of irritation.

e. Anger-control/out: controlling angry feelings by preventing the expression of anger toward other persons or objects.

f. Anger-control/in: controlling suppressed angry feelings by calming down or cooling off.

2. **Novaco Anger Scale and Provocation Inventory (NAS-PI) (2003)**
   Novaco's anger scale distinguishes among cognitive, arousal, and behavioral components of anger and Provocation Inventory reflects five areas viz., disrespectful treatment, unfairness, frustration, annoying traits of others, and irritations.

3. **Buss and Perry's Aggression Questionnaire (1992)**
   The Aggression Questionnaire have four subscales, i.e., anger, hostility, physical, and verbal aggression.

4. **Multidimensional School Anger Inventory for Males (MSAI)**
   Smith et al., 1998 assesses the affective, cognitive, and expressive aspects of anger.

5. **Children's Inventory of Anger (ChIA)** (Nelson and Finch, 2000)
   This self-report inventory identifies the kinds of situations that provoke anger in particular children—as well as the intensity of their anger response. Nelson's scale has four subscales, i.e., frustration, peer relationships, physical aggression, relations with authority.

6. **Deffenbacher's Driving Anger Scale** (Deffenbacher et al., 1994).
   Driving Anger Scale was the first instrument developed to assess driving-related anger. There are two versions of the DAS, a 33-item long form and a 14-item short form. The DAS involves a variety of potentially anger-provoking driving situations.

7. **Pediatric Anger Expression Scale** (PAES) (Jacobs, Phelps and Rohrs, 1989).
   The PAES is a 10-item self-report scale and defines anger in terms of anger-in (directed inward), anger-out (anger expressed outward),

anger control (focusing on maintaining control of anger reactions), and anger reflection (focus on cognitive resolution of stimulus event conflict).

8. Snell et al. (1995) in their **Clinical Anger Scale** described various symptoms of anger as:

    a. anger now,
    b. anger about the future,
    c. anger about failure,
    d. anger about things,
    e. angry-hostile feelings,
    f. annoying others,
    g. angry about self,
    h. angry misery,
    i. wanting to hurt others,
    j. shouting at people,
    k. irritated now,
    l. social interference,
    m. decision interference,
    n. alienating others,
    o. work interference,
    p. sleep interference,
    q. fatigue,
    r. appetite interference,
    s. health interference,
    t. thinking interference, and
    u. sexual interference.

Figure 1.9 Spielberger STAXI-2

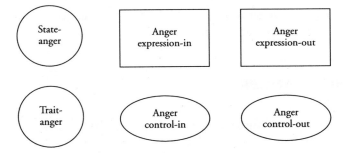

TYPES OF ANGER

According to Obstaz (2008) there are eight types of anger:

1. *Chronic anger*—ongoing resentment toward others and life in general.
2. *Volatile anger*—comes and goes, builds to rage, explodes as physical or verbal aggression.
3. *Judgmental anger*—critical statements are made which belittle, shame, or correct others, done with disdain.
4. *Passive anger*—expressed indirectly through sarcasm, or being late, or avoiding a situation.
5. *Overwhelming anger*—arises when people can't handle their life circumstances, and lash out to relieve stress or pain.
6. *Retaliatory anger*—directed to a person to get back at them for something that they did or said.
7. *Self-inflicted anger*—may result in hurting oneself emotionally or physically—negative self-talk, starvation, eating or drinking to excess.
8. *Constructive anger*—using anger to make some positive difference, such as becoming involved in a cause or movement for positive change.

Figure 1.10   Types of Anger

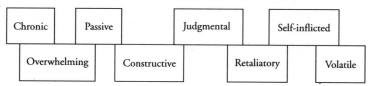

Other types of anger are direct anger-out, assertion, support seeking, diffusion, avoidance, and rumination (Linden et al., 2003).

MARITAL ANGER

Marital anger is a common phenomenon nowadays. Many love marriages are ending in divorce because of excessive anger and quarreling between partners. Anger in marriages is the leading cause of separation, child abuse, extra-marital affairs, conflicts, and even murders. Four types of anger expression have been defined in marriages (Mace, 1982).

- **Venting anger:** viewed as 'putting up a fight either verbally or physically'.
- **Suppressing anger:** described as 'avoiding the issue'.
- **Processing anger:** described as both parties sitting down to look at the situation objectively.
- **Dissolving anger:** described as the process of detaching oneself from the situation and accepting 'no concern about it nor involvement in it'.

Figure 1.11   Pictures of couples fighting

- There are many conflicting situations in married life such as adjustment problem, job stress, differential job status, money matters, controlling behavior, unemployment, sexuality, and other relationship matters, which in turn, have a strong relation with anger and aggression.
- Other factors can be previous unsuccessful relationships, inappropriate expectations, alcohol abuse, loss of trust, laziness, impatience, selfishness, pride, denial, dishonesty, lack of confidence, medical illness, extramarital affairs, and jealousy. Excessive television/video watching also leads to marital anger.
- Traditional belief that men are superior and should be the boss in the house, while women should obey, do the housework, and never refuse sex is also a significant cause of marital anger. Women inhibit the expression of anger because they have fear of rejection or loss of relationship while men do not anticipate such negative reaction (Campbell and Muncer, 1987).

- Experience of anger is common when attitudes of both partners are not matched and spouses blame each other for painful negative emotions.
- It is generally seen that partner who overreacts is unwilling to accept his/her reaction to marital difficulties and tend to criticize the partner.
- Spouses overreact with anger because of the failure to resolve resentment from past hurts with their spouses and other relationships.
- Such resentment is regularly released under stress and pressure.
- In this way, a vicious environment is formed in the family leading to everyday conflict, fights, jealousy, separation, and in extreme cases, murder also.
- About 1400 women, 30 percent of all murdered women, are killed by husbands, ex-husbands, and boyfriends each year; 2 million women are beaten; beatings are the most common cause of injury to 15 to 44-year-old women (Koss et al., 1994).
- Childhood experience of marital anger and aggression has a life long impact and interfere with other relationships in the life. Clinical experience indicates that in a marriage each partner has some degree of buried anger that they bring to the relationship. One out of every eight married men is physically aggressive toward his wife and nearly 2 million women are severely assaulted by their male partners (Straus and Gelles, 1990).
- Some people blame excessively and exclusively their spouse for their anger. This is especially the case when there has been childhood emotional trauma with parents.
- Marriages are becoming hell for many due to the everyday marital conflicts.
- Many people stay in marriage under pressure and ultimately many of them end divorced or commit suicide.

Figure 1.12 Unhappy couple

The 'perfect wife' and 'perfect husband' are becoming angry, hostile, and aggressive (Fullerton, 1977 cited in Tucker-Ladd, 2006).

- People find it difficult to have freedom and self-growth due to rigid behavior of their partners.

- Most often, marital anger is displaced toward other family members such as in-laws, grandparents, and children.
- Anger displaced toward children is very harmful because they have no way to escape.
- Therefore, for a healthy married life, there is a need for healthy expression of anger between spouses.

GENDER AND ANGER EXPRESSION

Gender roles affect a number of aspects in our lives. Emotional expression including anger is one of such aspect. Research in gender difference in expression of anger is conflicting. 'These gender difference in anger expression may be due to developmental or socialization differences among boys and girls.'

Social upbringing of boys and girls affects anger expression (Anderson and Lawler, 1995; Brody, 1996; Howells and Day, 2002; Piko, Keresztes, and Pluhar, 2006).

- It is generally seen that girls are socialized to be nice, not to be angry at any cost. Generally, females are expected to be emotional, sensitive, and nurturing in interpersonal relationships, which differentiate them from males in their behaviors.
- Throughout their development, girls internalize their negative feelings because they are aware that anger expression is likely to result in social rejection and emotional distress.

PARENTAL REACTIONS TO ANGER

- Anger is found to be appropriate for boys than for girls and parents are found to have more acceptance of anger in boys than in girls.
- Boys are encouraged to act out their angry feelings while girls are encouraged to keep down their angry feelings. In American culture anger generally is viewed as more appropriate for males than females (Kollar et al., 1991).
- Girls suppress their negative emotions. These strong feelings become toxic when kept inside. This suppressed feeling then finds other alternatives in the form of resentment, hostility, suspicion, impulsive, and other physiological irregularities.

- These suppressed feelings are the important factors in relational aggression, marital conflicts, and also the root cause of other family, social, and workplace disturbances at later stages of life.
- It is generally found that fathers accept or even reward girls for expression of sadness and fear, but punish boys for the expression of the same emotions.
- Mothers become more negative about aggression in their daughters and more tolerant to aggression in their sons, as children grow (Stevenson-Hinde, 1999; Mills and Rubin, 1992).
- Mothers identify young children being upset as 'sad' if the child is a girl, and 'mad' if the child is a boy (Fivush, 1989; Kuebli and Fivush, 1992).

Box 1.3   Differences by gender in expressions of anger due to social factors

- Girls are supposed to be emotional, sensitive, and nurturing in interpersonal relationships.
- Girls are socialized to be nice, not to be angry at any cost.
- Girls internalize their negative feelings to prevent social rejection and emotional distress.
- Girls are encouraged to keep down their angry feelings.

- The suppressed feeling finds other alternatives in the form of resentment, hostility, suspicion, impulsive, and other physiological irregularities.
- Aggression causes marital conflicts and is also the root cause of other family, social and workplace disturbances at later stages of life.
- Assertive women are not popular at work.

Box 1.4   Parental reactions to anger

- Mothers become more negative about aggression in their daughters and more tolerant of aggression in their sons.
- Mothers identify young children being upset as 'sad' if the child is a girl, and 'mad' if the child is a boy.

- Parents are more accepting of anger in boys.
- Boys are encouraged to act out their angry feelings. Boys often express their anger in violent behavior.
- Fathers accept or reward girls for expression of sadness and fear, but punish boys for the expression of these same emotions.

ANGER EXPRESSION DIFFERS IN BOTH GENDERS

- Girls are more verbally expressive of their emotions while boys express their emotions by acting out in harmful ways such as hitting, throwing, and breaking things, etc. (Lohr et al., 1988).
- Under anger inducing situation, boys are more likely to directly vent their anger, but girls are more likely to use coping strategies that are less inflammatory (Fabes and Eisenberg, 1992).
- Typical anger-response styles of males and females differ due to gender-role expectations (Labouvie-Vief et al., 2003).
- Boys tend to vent their angry feelings by physical activities while girls usually spent their time being alone or talking to someone close (Taylor and Novaco, 2005).
- Recent studies show that girls may feel more angry than boys. This may be because girls are more aware of their emotions or that they face more angry situations than boys do (Saini, 2006a).

GENDER IN A WORK PLACE ENVIRONMENT

- Assertive women managers are perceived less positively by both men and women coworkers, and are more socially isolated (Wiley and Eskilson, 1982; Raikkonen et al., 1992).
- Therefore, there are few opportunities for assertive women compared to those who suppress their anger.
- Since women are generally refrained from anger expression, they tend to suppress their anger which is directed to other feelings and therefore are more likely than men to express hurt feelings (Avrill, 1983).
- There are greater perceived benefits of anger for men than women (Howells and Day, 2002). Men get angrier than women because they have a greater sense of power and control and express their angry feeling in everyday life activities at home, public place, and workplace.
- While working on the benefits of anger, it is found that men often express the opinion that anger is seen as sexually attractive by women (Cummins, 2006).
- Both men and women expressed more feelings of anger when incited by the opposite sex (Frodi, 1977).

There are three major areas of gender differences in adult men and women (Taylor and Novaco 2005; Dave et al., 2006).

The Expression of anger

Males are more likely to express anger physically while women do so verbally.

The Situation

Males are more likely to express their anger outside home and to people they are not connected to, while females are more likely to express anger in the home and to loved ones.

The Antecedent for the anger

Males are more likely to respond angrily to behavior that they perceive as harmful and to physically aggressive females, while females are more likely to respond angrily to verbal aggression and insensitive or condescending behavior.

There appear to be some clear distinctions between men's expressions of anger and women's expressions of anger (Dave et al. 2006).

MEN'S ANGER

Men's perspective on men's anger: Men lash out, threaten, do not forgive nor forget, play physical games to get their own back, and hold grudges.

Women's perspective on men's anger: Men will sulk, get physical, threaten, become sarcastic, go drinking; they will make you stay and listen, and drive the car fast.

WOMEN'S ANGER

Women's perspective on women's anger: Women will ignore the other person, talk with friends about the situation, withdraw sex, self-harm, scream, pull hair/scratch, bring irrelevant issues into the situation, and spend on his credit card.

Men's perspective on women's anger: The bigger the problem the louder women will argue, they will bring up things from the past, little things will annoy them, they will give you the silent treatment, will cry, and will refuse to cook for you.

Box 1.5   Differences in anger expression by gender

Women	Men
▪ Verbally expressive of their emotions.	▪ Physical violence.
▪ Use coping strategies.	▪ Directly vent their anger.
▪ Like to be alone or talk to someone.	▪ Do physical exercise.
▪ Women are generally refrained from expressing anger.	▪ Men are angrier than women: more sense of power and control.
▪ Therefore, they tend to suppress their anger and are displaced in the expression of other feelings.	▪ Express their angry feeling in everyday life activities at home, public place, and workplace.

Figure 1.13   Difference in anger expression by gender

GENDER IDEOLOGY

'Gender ideology refers to beliefs about appropriate sex roles for each gender.'

Traditional gender ideology

- Individuals with traditional gender ideologies believe that men should be the breadwinner and head of the family and that woman should maintain the household and family relationships, rear children, and play supportive roles to men (Wilkie et al., 1998).
- Traditional gender ideology places men's identities within work and accords them more power in the family, and places women's identities at home and in familial roles and accords them less power than their male partners (Hochschild et al., 1989).

Egalitarian gender ideology

- An egalitarian gender ideology holds that men and women should have equal status both at home and workplace, and equally share responsibility for housework and childcare. An egalitarian gender ideology bases men and women's identities on the same tasks in the same sphere, thereby according each equal power in relationships (Hochschild et al.1989).
- It is generally found that women, younger people, people with more education and income have a more egalitarian attitude to gender roles.

Women report more anger than men; more the number of children there are in a household, the greater the anger among adults, especially women; and the divorced report more anger than the married, widowed, and never married. These can be attributed to gender inequities in domestic labor and childcare, and economic hardships associated with gender inequality (Ross and Willigen, 1996).

Figure 1.14   Traditional gender ideology

CHILDHOOD ANGER

Childhood is the most important stage of human development. Experts are of the view that anger develops more often in the family, in relation with marriage, and in bringing up children than in any other human relationship. There is nothing wrong in feeling angry. The only concern is appropriate expression (Eastman and Rozen, 1994).

Everyday children see episodes of anger at home, school, public places, on television, and video games. Children face many emotional problems in relation to identity crises, separation, frustration, confusion, embarrassment, loneliness, isolation, anxiety, etc., during this period of development. Visual media adds to it, as it is an important source of learning anger.

The common characteristics of child anger have been suggested below. The more characteristics that match the child, the more likely he/she will have a problem with anger (Eastman and Rozen, 1994).

- Blow-ups when pressure builds,
- can't handle change or stress,
- shows rage when troubled by pain, loss, hurt, frustration, or disappointment,
- can't calm down when angered,
- fights with others frequently,
- uses words as weapons,
- blames others,
- turns anger into shouting,
- tantrums or aggression,
- thrives on revenge,
- will not take responsibility,
- lacks self-control,
- has a low self-confidence,
- doesn't appear to care about others' feelings or rights,
- won't compromise, and
- can't negotiate.

The following are some other characteristics of anger in children (Trama and Saini, 2005).

- Children do not have skills or self-control for managing their behaviors.
- Children continuously need guidance about how to control and appropriately express their emotions.
- With extreme anger, the child can become totally consumed by angry thoughts and feelings. He or she may be unable to stop screaming, or in some cases, acting out physically by hitting, throwing things, yelling, slamming doors, and fighting with others.

- Anger can make children drop out of school.
- A child is angry when pressure builds or when stressed, or when faced with a loss, or when hurt.
- Anger can also come when there is feeling of blame, or revenge, low self-confidence, frustration, and disappointment.
- Children with angry feelings are more risk takers and have poor impulse control. They enjoy more physical play than their peers and like taking chances.
- Children who do not manage anger are at higher risk of weight gain, food addiction, drug abuse, aggression, hypertension, diabetes, cancer, etc. (Knox et al., 1998; Scherwitz and Rugulies, 1992; Thomas et al., 2000).
- Children often are self-centered and cannot consider the other's point of view while reacting.
- Children often do not care about others feeling and do not take responsibility of their actions.
- Children who expressed their anger to a moderate degree were much less likely to have adjustment problems, especially externalizing problems, compared with children who expressed their anger either too much or too little (Cole et al., 1996).

FAMILY STRUCTURE AND EFFECT ON ANGER

Family is the first school of learning behaviors. Family is the primary source for socializing emotional expression because an individual first communicates his or her needs and desires within the family. Family structure and family change have a significant impact on a child's well being (Halberstadt and Eaton, 2003; Saarni and Buckley, 2002).

'Parents can pro-vide a marvelous environment of love and encouragement as well as arenas for anger and aggression.'

CONSTANT PARENTAL FIGHTS HAVE ADVERSE EFFECTS ON CHILDREN

- With the changing socialization practices, families are getting shrunk. More and more dual-earner and nuclear families are coming up.

- Children of working parents are also likely to develop some deviant behaviors because they may not get proper parental attention and guidance in everyday problems. Such children seek sensations in deviant behaviors such as fast driving, drinking, strikes, fights, and in control behaviors. These children express their feelings

Figure 1.15 Childhood exposure to parental aggression

by kicking, screaming, swearing, hitting, or throwing things. They do not know other ways to express their angry feelings that can get them parental attention.

- Due to increased professional responsibilities and other problems such as differential views of parents, marital discord, etc., and inappropriate communication between elders and children, families are becoming more disturbed.
- Changes in family such as parental separation, single parenthood, remarriage, dual earner parents, nuclear family, and joint family have a wide variety of adverse effects on child development. These adverse impacts may include hostile behavior, conduct behavior, schooling, peer relations, anger, aggression, violence, smoking, drinking, eating disorders, gambling, road rage, early sexual onset, teenage pregnancy, and even risk of STDs like HIV/AIDS.
- Children whose parents are separated face many adjustment problems and social conduct problems. Such children inhibit their emotions and thus an emotional turmoil makes him angry, hostile, and aggressive.
- Children from divorced families have higher rates of externalizing behavior problem (Emery et al., 1999).
- Among children who had experienced a parental separation, those whose parents reconciled or whose mother remarried exhibited more behavioral difficulties than children who remained in a single-parent family (Fergusson et al., 1986).
- Boys with divorced parents, where both parents exhibit competent parenting behaviors, are at no greater risk of involvement in delinquent behavior than boys living in an intact family (Simons et al., 1999).

Figure 1.16   Family factors and anger generation

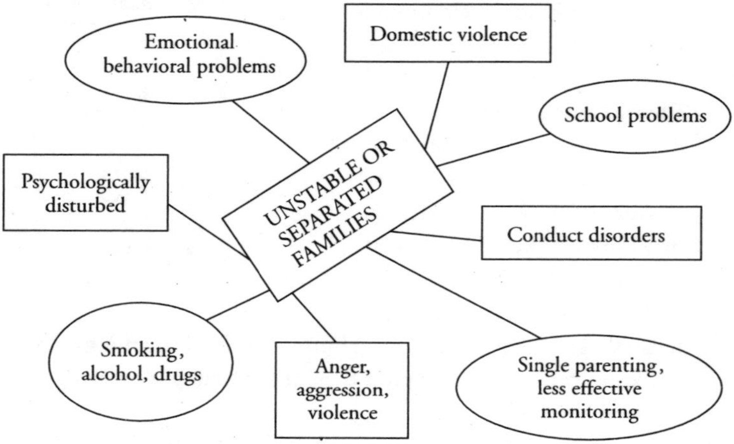

Figure 1.17   Effect of angry parents on children

ANGRY PARENT → ANGRY FAMILY ENVIRONMENT → ANGRY CHILD

Figure 1.18   Boy being scolded by his father and then the boy fighting with his friend

In undesirable dating situation an adolescent may respond to anger in a way that they have learned from their parents.

EFFECTS OF DOMESTIC VIOLENCE

Domestic violence is increasing in all societies world over. It has a direct effect on young children. Social learning theory says that children may learn anger expression styles from observing how people around them respond to anger (Bandura, 1973).

Figure 1.19   Child exposed to marital conflict

- Children exposed to marital conflicts are more likely to exhibit high risky behaviors including angry outbursts in their everyday activities (Cummings and Davies, 1994).
- Child abuse and child maltreatment in families leads to the development of an angry temperament in children.
- Children exposed to frequent parental conflicts at home become more prone to adult anger (Cummings et al. 1989).
- Conflict between parents, whether in intact or divorced families, is a risk factor for externalizing and internalizing behavior problems, low school achievement and low social competence (Cummings and Davies, 1994; Grych and Finchum, 1990).
- Adolescents report stronger negative reactions, including anger, fear, sadness, and shame when exposed to increasing intensity of adult conflict (Grych and Finchum, 1990).

PARENTING STYLE AND ANGER GENERATION

This has a strong relation with childhood anger. Different parenting styles including authoritative, authoritarian, and permissive-indulgent and permissive-indifferent, along with other parental attributes and practices nourish certain behaviors in children, which in turn, lead to disruptive behavior including anger and aggression (Maccoby and Martin, 1983).

There are some other parental factors, that may predispose children to behave angrily and these may include family size, parental education, maltreatment, child abuse, punishment, parental illness, and parental aspirations. Parenting styles that often correspond with children's excessive anger are 'giving too much' or 'giving too little' (Namka, 1997).

CHILD ABUSE AND ANGER GENERATION

- *The* 'giving too much' *parent* tries to meet the child's every need. This results in the child believing that the world revolves around him. Some children who are badly spoiled by their parents grow up believing that they should get everything they want and they have the right to be angry if they do not get it. This parenting style results in a high demand child who does not learn to deal with inner frustration and delay in gratification.
- *The* 'giving too little' *parent* is self-involved and does not nurture the child. The parent may be cold and rejecting, due to being involved with addictions or being an angry person himself. The parent may be busy and self-involved. A child in such environment grows up feeling neglected, rejected, and abandoned. Every day he must contend with feelings of desperation, being misunderstood, frustration, fear, loss, grief, and betrayal. Such children cannot express their anger because they fear that their parents might reject them further (Namka, 1997).

Figure 1.20 Mother scolding daughter for scoring low in an exam

A child who is heavily criticized and abused by a parent often grows up believing 'damned if I do and damned if I don't'. This type of child feels that he is not worthy of getting his needs met and feels ashamed for not measuring up to what his parent expects of him, even though it may be irrational. The child who suffers from verbal and physical abuse is angry about this injustice. His hostility toward others is displaced anger (Namka, 1997).

Parents play a crucial role in emotional socialization of children. How parents treat their children, whether with harsh discipline or warmth, has deep and long lasting consequences for the child's emotional life (Goleman, 1995).

IMITATION

- Children learn how to deal with their feelings of anger by imitating the behavior of their parents.
- Children learn by watching what adults do and behave accordingly.
- If children often experience anger within their families, they are more likely to behave in a similar way in the future.

POOR EMOTIONAL BONDAGE IN THE FAMILY

- Emotional attachment in children is an important phenomenon and relates to emotional regulation.
- Children with secured attachment openly express their emotions and are more skillful in emotional regulation (Bus and van Ijzendoorn, 1988, 1995).

POOR ANGER MANAGEMENT IN PARENTS (TRAMA AND SAINI, 2005)

- Parents, who do not care to teach their children about anger management, will raise children who are likely to be angry, hostile, disappointed, frustrated, and aggressive.
- Children learn a lot of experience, beliefs and values from the family members. Anger is most frequently reported emotion by parents while care-taking of children.
- When family members have conflicts, have distorted views, abuse, and blame each other and children see that their parents are tolerating such behaviors in silence, children learn to do the same when anger is directed toward them.

- On the other hand, when they see destructive parental reaction to angry feelings, they also learn such behavior (Tavris, 1989). Children often show such behavior at home by breaking things, and at school by fighting with peers, and these are lined with aggressive elementary schooling (Tavris, 1989).

PARENTS USING A GREAT DEAL OF PUNISHMENT

Harsh physical punishment from parents is a strong predictor of children's aggression and makes children more rigid and aggressive in nature. Research has shown that harsh physical discipline by parents was associated with increased peer victimization, and such children were found to be engaging in aggressive fantasies, which in turn, was associated with higher levels of aggression (Weiss et al., 1992).

Figure 1.21   Child abuse

- Mothers who rely heavily on physical punishment promote defiant and impulsive children (Larzelere, 2000).
- If parents continuously threaten children and scold them, the children will continue to misbehave and get scolded and threatened further. Straus (1993) found that parents who, in their childhood, had been physically punished beyond the age of 13 were more likely to severely assault or abuse their own children.
- This cycle continues and a child develops angry feelings and aggressive behavior at home, school, and society.

- The child born and raised in such an angry environment becomes an angry adult, thus giving rise to a vicious cycle.
- Therefore, it is a parent's responsibility to provide opportunity for children to learn frustration, tolerance, and effective problem solving techniques.

Be cautious since physical punishment may teach that violence is an acceptable way to solve problems.

URBAN VS RURAL ENVIRONMENT

Location is also a significant factor in expression of anger among children. It has been found that urban children easily express their negative emotions as compared to suburban- and rural-area children. Ross and Roberts (1999) found that 40 percent of children in low-income families demonstrate high levels of indirect aggression, as compared to 25 to 29 percent of children in families whose incomes are $30,000 or higher.

ADOLESCENT ANGER

World Health Organization defines adolescence as the age group of 10–19 years. The period of adolescence 'comprises a developmental process in which children move from the dependency and immaturity of childhood toward the physical, psychological, and social maturity of adulthood' (Goldstein and Glick, 1987).

Figure 1.22 Peer-relation anger

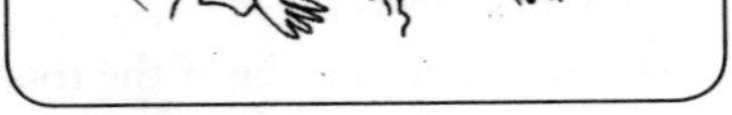

This phase is characterized by the following:

- Adolescents mature sexually and these physical developments affect behavior and emotions.

- Psychologically, adolescents desire independence and development of their identity, experience the tension of inner conflict while questioning the authority and values of their parents and others.
- Adolescents exhibit an inflated sense of responsibility and a strong need for adult approval.
- They desire to make their own decisions, like adults, but have not yet acquired the skills nor discipline necessary for effective and appropriate decision-making.

Some important characteristics of adolescents are peer pressure, increasing importance of friends, dating, body dissatisfaction, food addiction, very much concerned about what they wear and how they look. Other issues are a thrill-seeking behavior, temptation for physical attractiveness, indulgence in smoking, alcohol, drugs, sex and late night dance parties; adolescents often face identity crises.

CHARACTERISTICS OF ADOLESCENT ANGER (Goldstein and Glick, 1987)

- Adolescence is a difficult time for both parents and adolescents.
- Adolescents go through emotional turmoil and have angry feelings.
- They express their angry feelings through hostile behavior i.e., fighting, arguing, mood swings, depression, insomnia, loneliness, and social withdrawal.
- There is a direct relationship between high levels of anger and problem behavior at school, poor academic performance, peer rejection, aggression, violence, and psychosomatic complaints.
- First time juvenile crime offenses are being committed on the average at the age of 13 years; and this age is getting lower (Goldstein and Glick, 1987).
- Emotions may be at the root of their disruptive behavior and one of the emotions that cause much anxiety, hurt, disruption, and violence is anger.
- There are often continuous fights between parents and adolescents in the form of arguments, withdrawal on everyday issues, etc.
- Adolescents want to do things on their own and do not want any interference. Parental rules and values are often challenged or broken. This leads to parental anger and perpetuates anger in adolescents.

- At this stage of development, peer pressure is very influential on everyday activities. 'The peer group becomes a powerful influence and affects adolescents' behavior and attitudes' (Goldstein and Glick, 1987).
- When there is a parental interference in these activities, adolescents intensely resent their interference and develop negative feelings toward parents, which are displaced in angry outbursts to others.
- Adolescents engage in a wide range of antisocial activities, which have in their roots suppressed negative feelings. These may include hitting, stealing, damaging other's property, and setting fires.
- Therefore, adolescents need to receive appropriate direction, nurturing, encouragement, and guidance from significant adults for their successful transition into adult life and to protect them from developing negative emotions that may lead to anger, aggression, and violence.

PEER STRUCTURE AND ANGER

- Peers typically replace the family as the center of a young person's socializing and leisure activities.
- Peers may influence each other to engage in antisocial behavior. Anger has been associated with poor peer relationships and externalizing disorder in children and adolescents (Gjerde, Block, and Block, 1988).
- Teenagers have multiple peer relationships, and they confront multiple 'peer' cultures.
- Abusive dating relationship is the most frequent problem of adolescence. It has been found that most of the young children who date, suffered from violence including physical, psychological, and sexual abuse from their partners. Daily newspapers are filled with many cases of rape, suicides, and murders of girls because of their boyfriends and partners. Twenge and Quinlivan (2006) demonstrated that frustration with associates, friends, and loved ones has been identified as a major antecedent of anger.
- Peer pressure may encourage smoking, drug abuse, violence, delinquency, gangs, and school failure. Children who drink and use drugs are more likely to practice unprotected sex at an earlier age, have low self-esteem, suffer from school performance problems, and are more angry and aggressive.
- Day by day increasing family conflicts, economic hardship, and other family strains have made a distance between parents and children and children rely more on peers for emotional support.

- Unresolved issues between parents and children result in arguments, disagreements and withdrawal from the family. This further put young children at the risk of many psychological and other conduct problems including anger and hostile attitude toward others.
- Children who do not get emotional support in the family, get depressed easily and are poor at problem solving and come under peer pressure.
- Coercive family interactions including anger, conflict, and aggression are involved in generalization of conflict and aggression to peer domain (Thompson, 1994).
- Some reports suggest that poorly regulated anger often results in neurological impairment and mental disorders like learning disability and ADHD (Stevenson et al., 2002). Children with problems of learning disability and ADHD are more often rejected due to their age inappropriate behaviors and such children are likely to associate with delinquent peers to get acceptance and approval.
- Children who often demonstrate competent behavior in social situations with peers are thought to be skilled at social information processing, whereas children with social information processing deficits are more likely to experience chronic anger and act out in aggressive or socially inappropriate ways with peers (Trachtenberg and Viken, 1994).
- We like people who are like ourselves and dislike people who are different from us (Byrne, 1969). We naturally like people who reward us and dislike people who punish us, and similarity is rewarding. If groups are competitive, critical, and punishing of each other, the dislike and anger and aggression between the groups grow.

Figure 1.23   Peer group smoking and drinking

YOUTH ANGER

Youth anger is one of the most important aspects of human living and is associated with almost every physiological, psychological, social, national, and international problems.

Figure 1.24   Violence in teenagers

THE ANGER, HOSTILITY, AND AGGRESSION (AHA)-SYNDROME

Anger (*Dosh*), hostility (*Daveish*), and aggression (*Rosh*) collectively called the AHA-Syndrome is the leading cause of physical, physiological, and psychological problems among people of all ages (Saini, 2009; Tafrate et al., 2002).

- This is one of the leading causes of today's youth problems.
- This can lead to health problems like high blood pressure, diabetes, eating disorders, smoking, drinking, addictive behaviors, and stress related disorders.
- Sensation seeking leads to sex abuse, rape, murder, aggressive driving, and traffic accidents.
- Highly impulsive and sensation seeking youth do not consider the future outcome of their present behavior.
- Frustrations and depression give rise to high rates of suicidal ideation, suicide attempts, and suicides.
- Aggression and violence among youths are major problems for the family, society, and for the nation at large.
- Increasingly, newspapers and news channels are reporting rapes and murders by youth of a very young age. The root causes of such actions are suppressed angry feelings, which find their outlet in such heinous deeds.

Today's young generation is passing through a great change in society. Rich are becoming more rich and poor are becoming poorer. Youth from very rich and very poor sections of society demonstrate more high-risk behavior compared to children from middle-income group with stable families.

Therefore the only solution to break this syndrome is to stop blaming others, to stop turning it into hostility, and to stop its further development into aggression.

UNCONTROLLED ANGER

Anger is one of the most misunderstood emotions. When it is not expressed in an appropriate manner it can cause serious problems to individual, family, society, and nation at large.

- Anger can cause many physiological, psychological, and social problems when it is not expressed appropriately.
- An individual under the influence of anger cannot rationalize things, or take a right decision and hence always blames others.
- Psychologically, anger makes a person not able to function in an optimal mental faculty as it causes various negative emotions: anxiety, low frustration level, unreasonable expectation, irrational perception, illogical reasoning, perceived threats, fear, and impulsivity.
- Anger can make an individual indulge in antisocial activities such as violence, damaging property, hurting others physically or verbally, etc.
- Anger destroys interpersonal relationships, affects marital relationships, causes mental illness, impairs judgment, and results in violent crimes, road rage, unsafe driving, and traffic accidents (Deffenbacher, 1993; Deffenbacher et al., 2003; Saini, 2009).

Therefore, if anger is not controlled it is harmful at all levels of developments.

Figure 1.25 Social effects of anger

CAUSES OF ANGER

EFFECTS OF SOCIAL FACTORS ON ANGER EXPERIENCE AND EXPRESSION

Social factors are an important source of anger experience and expression.

Social anger is generated by social issues like social inequality and social constraints, which are frequently seen in today's unfair world. Such types of social anger make good news material and are frequently covered in great detail by various news channels and newspapers.

'Social inequality' always leads to anger in socially disadvantaged people. Some such issues are e.g., reservation issues, price hikes in daily use commodities such as petrol, religious issues, portraying of a film that hurts sentiments, unemployment issues, civil rights, war, and terrorism, including other political and legal decisions.

- Social anger expression includes protests, strikes, agitation, fights, damage to public property, etc.
- Anger is a product of social life, people get angry when treated unfairly or when others fail to fulfill a social contract (Hegtvedt and Markovsky, 1995; Smith-Lovin, 1995; Ross and Van Willigen, 1996).

'Social structure' also affects people's belief about the world and their ability to deal with their problems.

- The ongoing conflicts in our country at the borders for the possession of Kashmir valley, 'Narmada Bachao Andolan' in Gujarat against building a dam, agitation against many other social sanctions for the 'people' are causing a lot of anger and in some severe cases, leading to mass destruction of property and people.
- It has been found that youngsters from socially disadvantaged locations are most engaged in antisocial activities such as gambling, smuggling of drugs, theft, rape and murder, which have their root in negative emotions, including anger.
- People in socially disadvantaged location have fewer personal resources, such as self-efficacy (Hughes and Demo, 1989), social resources such as social integration (Pearlin and McKean, 1996) to enable them to manage their difficulties. Hence socially disadvantaged people have poor emotional regulation and management of their emotions. These people face many unfair treatments and barriers to their achievements, which is displaced in angry outbursts.

- Anger resulting from many experiences of perceived discrimination or other non-personal, systemic forms of unfair treatment might be repressed or displaced onto close others until or unless a catalyzing experience provokes a release, as in 'black rage' (Grier and Cobbs, 1968) and 'social rage' (Berry, 1999).

Poverty

There is a vicious circle linking poverty and ill health including physical and psychological health. Poverty leads to more crimes for example, a higher incidence of drug and alcohol abuse, higher incidences of teenage pregnancy, and more violent crime (Jargowsky, 1994).

- Lack of adequate recreational resources, financial deficits, and improper home/social environments often make such people chronically angry and they resort to unhealthy behaviors like gambling, stealing, aggression, violence, unsafe sex, and other deviant behaviors.

EFFECTS OF BEHAVIORAL FACTORS ON ANGER EXPRESSION

Behavioral factors contribute to anger expression in many everyday life situations.

- It is generally seen that angry people create an atmosphere or environment in which others respond with anger, creating a cycle of anger.
- Inflammatory statements and personal attacks are also the causes of general anger expression during a normal discussion.
- When people are told it is them who are at fault for a particular situation, or that they are wrong or stupid in believing something or advocating a particular action, the person attacked is likely to respond in a very negative way. In such situations, they are more likely to refuse to listen to the other side's arguments and behave more angrily.

Figure 1.26 Anger and its effects on others

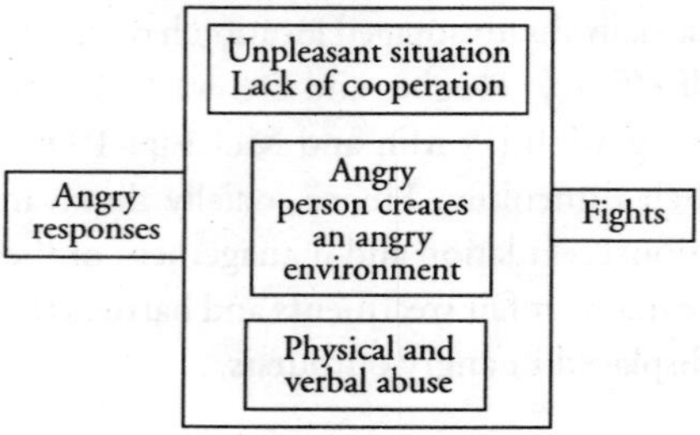

EFFECTS OF BELIEFS, EXPECTATIONS, AND DEMANDS ON ANGER EXPRESSION

'Beliefs and expectations are two important sources of emotions in human beings.' They are the important arbiters of perceptions of fairness and equity, and these perceptions are closely tied to anger.

- Beliefs about what is fair determine what people expect, how they construe events, and what they perceive as fair and equitable.
- When people get what they expect, they are less likely to respond to injustice (Hegtvedt and Markovsky, 1995).

'Expectations are something that we long to happen.'

- Expectations usually develop when we compare ourselves with others or they stem from promises people make.
- Expectations may be about future, about our needs in our lives like being loved, accepted, and feeling safe. When these expectations are not met, people react in anger.
- People unrealistically behave in anger when others do not behave according to them and situations do not turn out accordingly. Violation of expectation of fairness leads to anger and dissatisfaction (Hetgvedt and Markovsky, 1995).
- This often leads an angry person to blame others and have angry outbursts against them.
- It is natural to get angry when obstacles are put in the path of our goals or desires.
- When people make demands, they see things as how they should be and not as they really are. This lowers their tolerance and this becomes the cause of anger expression. When things do not go their way, they feel frustrated and hence react.

Figure 1.27   Causes of anger

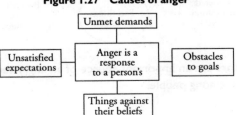

EFFECTS OF PHYSICAL HEALTH ON ANGER EXPRESSION

Physical health has a direct relationship with anger expression:

- Anger is a common result of chronic pain and discomfort in everyday life situation.
- People with physical illness or discomfort such as headaches, fatigue are frustated with their pain and react in anger. Children with severe physical illness suppress their angry feelings that add to their distress (Steele et al., 2000).
- It is a general tendency that when we are uncomfortable due to any physical problem or illness, we are not in control and tend to get angry even at our parents, children, and beloved.
- There are many examples of such anger expression in hospitals. Doctors and nurses usually face such anger from patients suffering through physical pain.
- Pain whether physical or emotional, lowers our frustration tolerance and becomes the cause of anger.

Figure 1.28   Anger and ill health

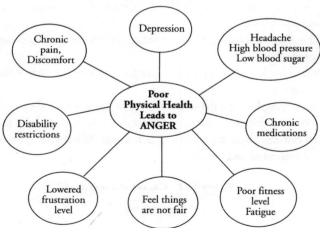

Biological factors are an important source of an angry temperament and aggression among people.

These include high blood pressure, hypoglycemia (low blood sugar), high testosterone (male sex hormone), brain damage, and irregularities of neurotransmitters, genetic defects, heredity, immune system, and other hormonal changes in the body.

INFLUENCE OF ALCOHOL AND DRUGS ON ANGER

Alcohol impairs reasoning and other brain functions and brings out behaviors that are normally repressed.

- High levels of anger are found to be associated with high levels of adolescent alcohol use (Hussong and Chassin, 1994).
- Intoxication is very closely linked with acts of violence (Murdoch et al., 1990). In adults, anger-out has been implicated in excessive drinking and smoking (Davidson et al., 2000).
- A positive correlation exists between the quantity of alcohol consumed and the frequency of a wide variety of violent acts, including sexual assault, child abuse, and homicide.
- Alcohol and drugs affect how our brain processes information and can make a person more irritable with a low threshold that can trigger violent anger.

MENTAL HEALTH AND ANGER

'Mental health is a challenging health issue nowadays at almost every stage of life.'

- Mental health problem interferes with the normal development of the children and adolescents and results in many serious consequences, thereby reducing capacity of society and productivity of a whole nation.
- Some common mental health issues among adolescents are anger, hostility, aggression, anxiety, stress, depression, impulsivity, eating disorders, poor self-esteem, suicidal ideation, etc.
- Low income causes depression in families and most importantly in mothers and depressed mothers bring up depressed and angry children.

LEARNING DISABILITY AND ANGER

'Learning disability is a heterogeneous group of disorders manifested by significant difficulties in the acquisition and use of listening, speaking, reading, writing, reasoning, or mathematical skills.' Learning disability affect the way an individual takes in, remembers, and understands information, and how the person expresses that knowledge.

- People with learning disability are likely to be hyperactive, restless, impulsive, forgetful, and have poor problem solving abilities. A core element of challenging behavior in people with learning disabilities is failure to control anger (Black et al., 1997).
- These characteristics of learning disability make them angry and aggressive in their everyday activities.

CHILDREN WITH ADHD

All children behave angrily/aggressively from time to time but it is more common for children with ADHD (Attention Deficit Hyperactivity Disorder). Recently it has been found that individuals diagnosed with ADHD in childhood reported elevated levels of anger, physical and verbal aggression (Harty et al., 2009).

- The problems of hyperactivity, inattention, and impulsivity in children interfere with their interaction with others, leading to anger and aggression.
- Hyperactivity causes a child to talk excessively, run excessively, play too roughly, and hurt other children.
- Inattention causes poor attention and children suffering from this do not listen to requests by others.
- Impulsive children act out quickly without thinking and have volatile moods resulting in angry outbursts and aggression.

EMOTIONS AND ANGER

'Emotional reasoning is one of the important characteristics of emotional development. Emotions play an important role in development of anger' (Spielberger et al., 1995).

- Gottman, Fainsilber-Katz, and Hooven (1997) described parental influences on the children's regulation of emotion and stressed that parents recognize and validate children's emotional states, help children label them, and help children resolve the situations that lead to explosive emotional display.
- People who reason emotionally can misinterpret normal events and things as being directly threatening to their needs and goals.
- People who use emotional reasoning tend to become irritated and react angrily.
- There are many emotions such as anxiety, stress, depression, dependency, guilt, jealousy which have a complex relationships with anger.
- When people are anxious, feeling guilty, stressed, or under depression, they are likely to respond in anger.

FRUSTRATION TOLERANCE

Frustration tolerance is the ability of a person to continue on a task when frustration occurs due to setbacks and difficulties.

- Common factors that lower our frustration tolerance are stress, anxiety, depression, physical or mental pain, alcohol and drugs, irritations, etc.
- Everyone faces frustration when his or her goals or desires get blocked. The level at which a person gets frustrated by a particular event or task is called that person's frustration level.
- Sometimes our ambitions exceed our abilities and that becomes the cause of frustration, which in turn becomes the cause of anger.
- Most provocations can be seen as a type of frustration in which a person has been identified as the agent responsible for the failure to attain the goal.

Figure 1.29   Anger and frustration tolerance

- People with low frustration tolerance are likely to have high anger (Mahon et al., 2006).
- Frustration always breeds anger and anything blocking the path of fulfilling one's desire results in angry outburst (Berkowitz, 1993).

NEGATIVE EMOTIONS AND ANGER

There are many negative emotions like fear, helplessness, insult, disappointment, denial, hate, argument, jealousy, and sadness that can manifest as anger.

Figure 1.30 Negative emotions and anger

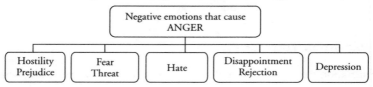

FEAR

'Fear and anger have been important tools to avoid and fight predators' (Adler, Rosen, and Silverstein, 1998).

- Anger is a defense mechanism for fear and people feel it is justified in that case.
- People are continuously living in the shadow of fear and therefore, are vulnerable to angry feelings and expression.
- While expressing anger, one moves from inside to outside and starts blaming others to find a solution to his/her internal fear.
- Television serials and movies are filled with horror movies and fear and it is generally portrayed that the hero fights for justice with anger and violence in such programs.

Emotions like fear and anger affect children's ability to relate to others

Adolescents who grow up in a family atmosphere of abuse and violence are more likely to alternate between roles of victim and victimizer, during conflict with peers or dating partners (Dodge, Pettit, and Bates, 1994).

Figure 1.31 Difficulty in emotional regulation

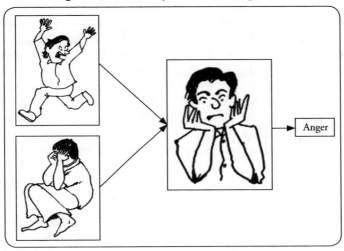

HOSTILITY

'Hostility the cognitive dimension of anger is negative behavior toward others and involves resistance, distrust, cynicism, critical attitude, gossips, resentment, hatred, withdrawal, etc.' All these negative emotions result in anger and aggression (Spielberger, 1983; Saini, 2009).

- Hostile people always remain irritable and aggressive. They experience high levels of stress and lower levels of social support due to their cynical nature and negative interaction with others (Smith, 1992).
- Buss (1961) suggested that hostility is negative cognitive appraisal of circumstances and individuals. Expressing hostility creates further hostility for others, thereby creating environment, which creates disturbance in the family, peer relations, school performance, and social learning.
- Children who have social skill deficit, lack basic skills in getting along with others, often respond with anger and aggression.
- Hostility is related with hyperactivity (Christensen and Smith, 1993) and has been found that those scoring high in hostility show exaggerated systolic blood pressures on stress reactivity (McCann and Matthews, 1988).

SHAME

Shame and anger have also been found to have a close relationship and this relationship has been supported by empirical findings (Hoglund and Nicholas, 1995). There are different views on whether women are more vulnerable to shame than males (Lewis, 1978).

- Inappropriate rage often has a strong relation with shame and is called *shame-rage spiral* (Kaufman, 1996; Retzinger, 1987).
- Shame renders the self passive and helpless, with power and agency being reclaimed through expressions of anger (Miller, 1985).

THREAT

Threat is also a common experience of living organisms, particularly human beings.

- Threat is a frequent cause of anger expression. Insult and threats to self-esteem have been proposed to trigger anger (Izard, 1977; Kemper, 1987).
- Anger is a natural response to threats. The belief in the ability to cope with potential threat causes anger (Frijda, 1986). That is, if the threat is strong than you, you experience fear and if you are stronger than the threat, you experience anger.
- Most of the times, it helps us in defending ourselves.
- There are many threatening situations when we are physically attacked and we respond with anger is such situations.

REJECTION

'Rejections are normal and commonly found in everyday human interaction.' People generally have difficulty in handling rejection and respond angrily.

- Rejection, whether from parents, peers, teachers, or classmates, have a strong relation with negative emotions that include anger, isolation, and discouragement. Peer rejection in early childhood is found to be predictive of aggression in late childhood (Dodge, Bates, and Pettit, 1990).

- Rejection in family and school for both children and adolescents and that in dating for adolescents lead to retaliation. Rejected people may desire revenge against those who reject them and express their need for revenge angrily. Their judgment and planning may deteriorate as these motives dominate their thinking (Leary, Twenge, and Quinlivan, 2006).
- Young children feel that the world is against them and this perceptual distortion makes them continue to behave aggressively. Buckley, Winkel, and Leary (2004) in an experimental study found that participants who received extremely rejecting feedback, reported high levels of anger than neutral or accepting feedback.
- When children do not get what they want from their parents, they try to fulfill their needs from others.
- Rejection in interpersonal relationships, specially in adolescents and young adults, often leads to addictive behaviors, alcohol, and drug abuse which have their roots in negative emotions.

EFFECTS OF BODY DISSATISFACTION

'Body dissatisfaction is a negative evaluation of one's figure and body parts. This can generate chronic anger in individuals' (Saini et al., 2008).

- Nowadays there is a growing dissatisfaction among adolescent boys and girls about their body image. Many go through it secretly as they have no one to trust and confide in about this sensitive matter.
- Body dissatisfaction is associated with emotional distress, which further makes the adolescents vulnerable to many psychological problems including stress, depression, irritability, anger, aggression, and eating disorders (Pinhas et al., 1999; Saini, 2006b).
- In almost every society, being thin is highly valued among women, whereas being slim and muscular is strongly appreciated among men.
- Studies have shown that approximately 60 percent of girls and 30 percent of boys report a desire to change their size or shape (Ricciardelli and McCabe, 2001; Wood et al., 1996) and nearly 25 percent of adolescent girls report clinically significant levels of body dissatisfaction (Stice and Whitenton, 2002).

- Children and adolescents with body dissatisfaction are likely to be more angry and have more negative feelings of both self and others, especially girls (Mueller et al., 2001; Saini et al., 2008).
- It has been found that adolescent girls who expressed their anger in a controlled, appropriate way had relatively few problems of excess body fat (Mueller et al., 2001).

Figure 1.32   Body dissatisfaction: a woman with a good figure perceives herself as fat when she looks in the mirror

EFFECTS OF VARIOUS PERSONALITIES AND PERCEPTIONS

TYPE-T PERSONALITY

'Type-T personality stands for thrill seeking behavior. Where thrill seeking is a personality trait in people who are risk takers and are motivated by variety, novelty, intensity, and uncertainty' (Farley, 1991).

- Type-T children seek activities that increase their adrenaline such as going fast on bicycles over ramps, jumping off from high places, and engaging in dangerous sports.
- They seem to have no fear of physical harm and are unaware of the danger in which they place themselves.
- They spend more time on the street and tend to get in trouble with others.

TEMPERAMENT

'Temperament is a typical style of behavior such as being emotional, intense, persistent, introvert, extrovert, impulsive, slow, fast, etc.'

- People who are extroverts are more likely to display aggression than introverts (Bates et al., 1985).
- Children who are fast in their actions are more likely to be aggressive than children who are slow.
- Sensitive people easily get hurt and are therefore more likely to be aggressive.
- An impulsive temperament often results in aggressive behavior.

IRRATIONAL PERCEPTION

People who get angry frequently have certain personality traits and thinking pattern.

- They have a certain perception and expectation of the world that they live in, and when in reality things do not meet their expectations, they become angry (Ellis, 1962; Lohr and Bonge, 1982).
- They usually blame their angry reactions on others and do not realize that they are angry because of their own irrational perception of the world.
- They have a set of beliefs that emphasize retaliation.
- They blame others for their problems and do not take responsibility for their own actions. They do not know how to break into their rigid thinking neither can they stop making judgments about others.
- They have strong 'shoulds' for others and get upset when others do not follow their wishes (Ellis, 1962).

Figure 1.33 Irrational perception and anger

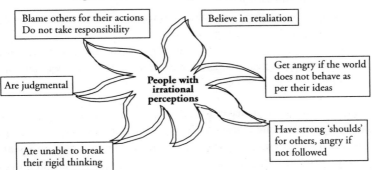

IMPULSIVITY

'Impulsivity means acting out without any planning. It is the failure to resist an impulse, drive, or temptation to perform an act that is harmful to others' (Barratt, 1994).

- Impulsive people are inclined to act on impulse rather than thought and are related with interpersonal aggression and crime (Lane and Cherek, 2000).
- They cannot resist their impulses and react instantly on slight provocation. Impulsivity in childhood has been related to poor anger control and aggressive behavior (Musher-Eizenman et al., 2004).
- There is a strong relation between impulsivity and anger/hostility (Barratt, 1994). Delinquent behavior is a result of deficits in impulse control (Barratt and Patton, 1983; Eysenck and Eysenck, 1977).

ENVIRONMENTAL FACTORS AND ANGER

'Environmental factors up to some extent have positive correlations in predisposing individual more prone to anger' (Wang et al., 2005). Environment includes home, office, personal space, territoriality, cultural groups, presence of aggressive cues, urban verses rural societies, social exclusion, etc.

Adverse environmental factors that can lead to anger are:

- *Home:* Noisy families, poor interpersonal relationships, marital discord and domestic violence.
- *Office:* Poor working conditions, unhygienic, noisy surroundings and discontent among colleagues.
- *Outdoor:* Extreme hot and cold weather, noise and air pollution, dirty roadsides, crowds and congestion on streets and driving through heavy traffic.

Adverse environment makes people vulnerable to stress, fatigue, anger, hostility, aggression, and other complaints, which further lead to many health problems. Such persons constantly express anger at home, office, and public places. Research has also shown that persons living in noisy neighborhoods tend to be more annoyed than persons living in quiet neighborhoods (Evans, Hygge, and Bullinger, 1995).

- People standing for hours in long lines can feel angry and aggressively break lines leading to fights.
- Drivers caught up in a traffic jam often react in anger by horn honking and shouting at others. Noisy horns make people aggressive while driving, resulting in risky driving, which is dangerous for both drivers and victims.
- Loud music at home or from neighborhood during exams or while sleeping is also a common experience of anger expression for both school-going children and elders.
- One study with a closer link to office environments found that high room temperature and air pollution were linearly linked to anger (Baron and Bell, 1975).
- Ozone levels and higher daily temperature have been found to be positively associated with family disturbances, as well as assaults against persons (Rotton and Frey, 1985).

Figure 1.34   Woman surrounded by loud noise and fighting children at home

Figure 1.35   A man with lot of noise in office

ANGER AND DRIVING

Drivers prone to high levels of anger also had higher rates of speeding, more erratic driving and tailgating, and twice as many crashes in these high impedance simulations (Deffenbacher et al., 2003). Arnett, Offer, and Fine (1997) found anger to be the only emotion that correlated with risky driving behaviors in adolescents.

Figure 1.36   Anger in Drivers

INTERNATIONAL ISSUES

International issues like war, terrorism, impacts of disasters, post traumatic stress disorder (PTSD), environmental stressors, poverty, ethnic and religious issues, spread of HIV/AIDS and other global epidemics also become the cause of anger expression in some or other ways.

- Bin Laden's anger toward America is one of the best examples of such kind. Laden's anger against the West is in opposition of 'unfairness', that is making people indulge in more heinous acts of humanity.
- There are so many demonstrations, strikes, and demands to manage these issues, which is a form of anger expression against such issues.

HARASSMENT

'Harassment is the physical or verbal behavior that interferes with work or creates an intimidating, hostile, or offensive work environment. People experience anger when they are harassed, assaulted, or attacked' (Spielberger and Sydeman, 1994).

- Harassment is generally done by people who are angry and dissatisfied in their own life.
- It can take many different forms, including intimidation or sexual harassment.

- Intimidation may include physical or verbal abuse, characterized by deliberate insults, threatening, and anger expression.

SEXUALITY

Sexual dysfunction and other related disorders are related to various emotional and behavioral problems including anger, hastility, and agression across the life. Some common sexual dysfunctions are inhibited sexual desire, dyspareunia, and orgasmic disorders.

- Disgusting or crude pornography increases aggression (Byrne and Kelley, 1981).
- Sexual harassment is also associated with the feelings of anxiety, anger, aggression, and poor self-esteem. Pornography and prostitution also have a positive link to anger expression.
- Sexual harassment includes offensive remarks of sexual nature, unwelcome advances, unwelcome requests for sexual favors linked to implied threats, or promises about career prospects, unwanted physical contact, visual displays of degrading sexual images, sexual assault, and rape. Sexual harassment is done by persons who are angry (Celik and Celik, 2007) and dissatisfied with various issues in life, including their sexual nature.

SPORTS ACTIVITIES

When sports are viewed as battles, the opponents become the enemy. Victory may encourage anger, aggression, and even violence among the fans. Some of the players are idolized by their fans just because of their aggression toward opponents.

Sports provide an opportunity for the expression of feelings and emotions (e.g. anger) which on the one hand may lead to improved mastering of stressful and emotionally charred situations, while on the other hand may lead to violent and aggressive behavior (Coakley, 1994). Sports such as cricket, hockey, boxing, and football contain a great deal of anger expression. Aggression in sports is often encouraged as part of 'winning at any cost'. This can have harmful effects on young minds.

Figure 1.37 Aggression and violence in sports

TIME MANAGEMENT

Time management is defined as managing our self in relation to time. It involves setting priorities and taking charge of your situation and time utilization.

- People who have effective time management do not feel hassled or 'on the edge' all the time, and thus can keep their calm.
- People who have poor time management and/or set unrealistic timetables and goals for themselves and their families or coworkers are always angry, as they are constantly stressed out meeting unmet deadlines.

Figure 1.38 Poor time management and anger

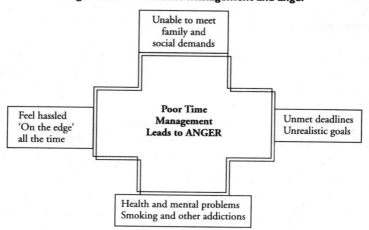

EFFECT OF MEDIA ON ANGER

Media is one of the most important sources of information and has a strong impact on today's living on almost every human being, especially children and adolescents. Media includes radio, television, movies, video, video games, newspapers, magazines, computer, mobiles, internet, and any gadget that provides information publicly. Basic emotions like anger, fear, love, enjoyment, sadness, surprise, shame, are often portrayed in the media and these are having a strong impact on the viewers especially at a young age. Media violence has affected people at almost every stage of life. Elementary school aged child is exposed to 8,000 murders and over 100,000 other acts of violence (Taylor et al., 1997).

Media arouses strong emotions, which leads to physiological changes and reactions. The effect of media on a person depends on the state of his or her emotional development.

Emotional development of a person takes place in five areas (Salovey and Mayer, 1990)

- ability in reading emotions,
- emotional self-awareness,
- harnessing emotions productively,
- managing emotions, and
- handling relationships.

Media has a strong influence in all these areas. If people are highly developed in these five areas and are emotionally sound or more field independent then they are less likely to be influenced by media portrayal of such emotions. They will have stronger and more appropriate emotional reaction to violence portrayed in media while exercising greater control over their personal behaviors in real life. Those who are more field dependent are likely to identify with such emotions and behave accordingly.

With greater experience with emotions, people are better equipped to make finer discriminations. Therefore, emotional intelligence matters a lot with regard to angry reactions among people.

The use of computer, internet, mobiles, and other forms of media has created revolutionary changes in various fields but on the other hand, the

Figure 1.39   Emotional development

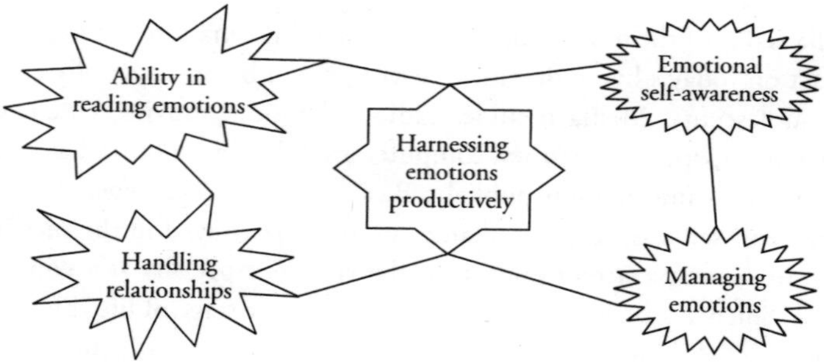

negative impacts are emerging in the form of many emotional and behavioral problems.

- The various factors that may influence development of angry reactions among people are children from lower classes and minority, the personality type, social milieu, racism, bigotry, eroticism, cognitive processing, emotional control, degree of identity, rewards and punishments, justification of violent acts, etc.
- All commercials on media including television, radio, magazines, newspaper, etc., are promoting perfect body, skinny, tall, beautiful girls, and creating a delusion among adolescents to be like that and to behave in the same manner.
- Teenagers struggle daily to look and dress like their idols shown in advertisements. This abnormal look is not physiological and not easy to achieve. This leads to feelings of inadequacy, depression, frustration, anger, and aggression. Young girls are most vulnerable to this. When they do not look like the beauty depicted in media, they get frustrated, angry, and end up feeling ugly and horrible (Saini and Trama, 2006).

SUMMARY

- Anger is a frequently occurring emotion, whose moderate to intense forms may be experienced several times a day by any individual (Averill, 1983).

- Anger may be evoked by a variety of external stimuli (e.g., persons, objects, and situations) or internal sensations (e.g., anger-laden memories, feelings of rejection, humiliation, and anxiety) that are interpreted as provocative and wrongful (Novaco, 2000).
- Anger experienced both internally and outwardly can be harmful, leading to both physiological and psychological problems.

Therefore, effective anger management techniques are required at every developmental stage and in every institution like family, school, and workplace. These have been discussed in a later section of the book.

REFERENCES

Adler, R. S., Rosen, B., and Silverstein, E. M. (1998). 'Emotions in Negotiation: How to Manage Fear and Anger', *Negotiation Journal*, 14(2): 161–79.

Anderson, C. A. (2000). 'Violence and Aggression', in A. E. Kazdin (ed.), *Encyclopaedia of Psychology* (pp. 162–69). Washington, DC: American Psychological Association and Oxford University Press.

Arnett, J. J., Offer, D., and Fine, M. A. (1997). 'Reckless Driving in Adolescence: 'State' and 'Trait' Factors', *Accident Analysis and Prevention*, 29: 57–63.

Averill, J. R. (1982). *Anger and Aggression: An Essay on Emotions*. New York: Springer-Verlag.

———. (1983). 'Studies on Anger and Aggression: Implications for Theories of Emotion', *American Psychologist*, 38: 1145–60.

Bandura, A. (1973). *Aggression: A Social Learning Analysis*. Oxford: Prentice-Hall.

Barkley, R. A. (1997). *ADHD and the Nature of Self-control*. New York: The Guilford Press.

Barratt, E. S. (1994). 'Impulsiveness and Aggression', in J. Monohan and H. J. Steadman, (eds.), *Violence and Mental Disorder*, (pp. 61–79). Chicago: University of Chicago Press.

Barratt, E. S., and Patton, J. H. (1983). 'Impulsivity: Cognitive, Behavioral, and Psychophysiological Correlates', in Zuckerman, M. (ed.), *Biological Bases of Sensation Seeking, Impulsivity*, and *Anxiety*, Lawrence Erlbaum Associates, (pp. 77–116). Hillsdale, NJ.

Baron, R. A., and Bell, P. A. (1975). 'Aggression and Heat: Mediating Effects of Prior Provocation and Exposure to an Aggression Model', *Journal of Personality and Social Psychology*, 31: 825–32.

Bates, J. E., Maslin, C., and Frankel, K. (1985). 'Attachment Security, Mother–Child Interaction, and Temperament as Predictors of Behavior Problem Rating at Age Three Years', in I. Bretherton and E. Waters (eds.), Growing Points of Attachment Theory and Research (pp. 167–93). *Monographs of the Society for Research in Child Development*, 50(1–2): 209.

Berkowitz, L. (1983). 'The Experience of Anger as a Parallel Process in the Display of Impulsive, "Angry" Aggression', in R. G. Geen and E. I. Donnerstein (eds). *Aggression: Theoretical and Empirical Reviews*, (Vol. 1). New York: Academic Press.

———. (1993). *Aggression: Its Causes, Consequences, and Control*. New York: McGraw-Hill.

Berkowitz, L., and Harmon-Jones, E. (2004). 'Toward an Understanding of the Determinants of Anger', *Emotion*, 4: 107–30.

Berry, B. (1999). *Social Rage: Emotional and Cultural Conflict.* New York: Garland Publishing.

Bhavisha, D., Pekkala, D., Allen, D., and Cummins, P. (2006). 'Gender and Anger' in Peter, C. (Ed.), *Working with Anger,* (pp. 149–58). England: John Wiley & Sons, Ltd.

Black, L., Cullen, C., and Novaco, R. W. (1997). 'Anger Assessment for People with Mild Learning Disabilities in Secure Settings', in B. S. Kroese, D. Dagnan, and K. Loumidis (eds.), *Cognitivebehaviour Therapy for People with Learning Disabilities.* London: Routledge.

Boergers, J., Spirito, A., and Donaldson, D. (1998). 'Reasons for Adolescent Suicide Attempts: Associations with Psychological Functioning', *Journal of the American Academy of Child and Adolescent Psychiatry,* 37: 1287–93.

Brody, L. R. (1996). 'Gender, Emotional Expression, and Parent–Child Boundaries', in R. D. Kavanaugh, B. Zimmerberg, and S. Fein (eds.), *Emotion: Interdisciplinary Perspectives* (pp. 139–70). Mahwah, NJ: Erlbaum.

Buckley, K., Winkel, R., and Leary, M. (2004). 'Reactions to Acceptance and Rejection: Effects of Level and Sequence of Relational Evaluation', *Journal of Experimental Social Psychology,* 40: 14–28.

Bus, A. G., and van Ijzendoorn, M. H. (1988). 'Mother–Child Interactions, Attachment, and Emergent Literacy: A Cross-sectional Study', *Child Development,* 59: 1262–72.

———. (1995). 'Mothers Reading to Their 3-year-olds—The Role of Mother–Child Attachment Security in Becoming Literate', *Reading Research Quarterly,* 30: 998–1015.

Bushman, B. J. (2002). 'Does Venting Anger Feed or Extinguish the Flame? Catharsis, Rumination, Distraction, Anger, and Aggressive Responding', *Personality and Social Psychology Bulletin,* 28: 724–31.

Buss, A. H. (1961). *The Psychology of Aggression.* New York: John Wiley.

Buss, A. H., and Perry, M. (1992). 'The Aggression Questionnaire', *Journal of Personality and Social Psychology,* 63: 452–59.

Byrne, D. (1969). 'Attitudes and Attraction', in L. Berkowitz (ed.), *Advances in Experimental Social Psychology:* Vol. 4 (pp. 36–90). New York: Academic Press.

Byrne, D. and Kelley, K. (1981). *An Introduction to Personality* (3rd ed.). Englewood Cliffs, NJ: Prentice-Hall.

Chinmayananda, Sw. (1976). *The Holy Geeta.* Bombay: Central Chinmaya Mission Trust.

Campbell, A., and Muncer, S. (1987). 'Models of Anger and Aggression in the Social Talk of Women and Men', *Journal for the Theory of Social Behaviour,* 17: 489–511.

Celik Y, Celik SS. (2007). 'Sexual Harassment against Nurses in Turkey, *Journal of Nursing Scholarship',* 39(2): 200–06.

Christensen, A. J., and Smith, T. W. (1993). 'Cynical Hostility and Cardiovascular Reactivity during Self-disclosure', *Psychosomatic Medicine,* 55: 193–202.

Coakley, J. (1994). *Sports in Society* (5th Edition). St. Louis: Mosby Year Book.

Cole, P. M., Zahn-Waxler, C., Fox, N. A., Usher, B. A., and Welsh, J. D. (1996). 'Individual Differences in Emotion Regulation and Behavior Problems in Preschool Children', *Journal of Abnormal Psychology,* 105: 518–29.

Crick, N. R., and Dodge, K. A. (1994). 'A Review and Reformulation of Social Information-Processing Mechanisms in Children's Social Adjustment', *Psychological Bulletin,* 115: 74–101.

Cummings, E. M., and Davies, P. (1994). *Children and Marital Conflict: The Impact of Family Dispute and Resolution.* New York: Guilford.

Cummings, J. S., Pellegrini, D. S., Notarius, C. I., and Cummings, E. M. (1989). 'Children's Responses to Angry Adult Behavior as a Function of Interparent Hostility', *Child Development,* 60: 1035–43.

Cummins, P. (2006). 'The Construction of Emotion', in C. Peter, (ed.), *Working with Anger*, (pp. 1–12). England: John Wiley and Sons, Ltd.

Davies, P. (1994). *Children and Marital Conflict: The Impact of Family Dispute and Resolution.* New York: Guilford.

Davidson, K., MacGregor, M. W., Stuhr, J., Dixon, K., and MacLean, D. (2000). 'Constructive Anger: Verbal Behavior Predicts Blood Pressure in a Population Sample', *Health Psychology*, 19: 55–64.

Deffenbacher, J. L. (1992). 'Trait Anger: Theory, Findings, and Implications', in C. D. Spielberger and J. N. Butcher (eds.), *Advances in Personality Assessment* (Vol. 9, pp. 177–201). Hillsdale, NJ: Lawrence Erlbaum.

Deffenbacher, J. L., Deffenbacher, D. M., Lynch, R. S., and Richards, T. L. (2003). 'Anger, Aggression, and Risky Behavior: A Comparison of High and Low Anger Drivers', *Behaviour Research and Therapy*, 41(6): 701–18.

Deffenbacher, J. L., Lynch, R. S., Filetti, L. B., Dahlen, E. R., and Oetting, E. R. (2003). 'Anger, Aggression, Risky Behavior, and Crash-related Outcomes in Three Groups of Drivers', *Behavior Research and Therapy*, 4(3): 333–49.

Deffenbacher, J. L., Oetting, E. R., and DiGiuseppe, R. A. (2002). 'Principles of Empirically Supported Interventions Applied to Anger Management', *The Counseling Psychologist* 2002; 30: 262–80.

Deffenbacher, J. L., Oetting, E. R., and Lynch, R. S. (1994). 'Development of a Driving Anger Scale', *Psychological Reports*, 74: 83–91.

Deffenbacher, J. L., Oetting, E. R., Thwaites, G. A., Lynch, R. S., Baker, D. A., and Stark, P. S. (1996). 'State-trait Anger Theory and the Utility of the Trait Anger Scale', *Journal of Counseling Psychology*, 43: 131–48.

DiGiuseppe, R., and Tafrate, R. (2006) *Understanding Anger Disorders*. New York, NY: Oxford University Press.

Dodge, K. A., Bates, J. E., and Pettit, G. S. (1990). 'Mechanisms in the Cycle of Violence', *Science*, 250: 1678–83.

———. (1994). 'Effects of Physical Maltreatment on the Development of Peer Relations', *Development and Psychopathology*, 6(1): 43–55.

Dodge, K. A., and Pettit, G. S. (2003). 'A Biopsychosocial Model of the Development of Chronic Conduct Problems in Adolescence', *Developmental Psychology*, 39: 349–71.

Dollard, J., Doob, L., Miller, N., Mowrer, O. H., and Sears, R. R. (1939). *Frustration and Aggression*. New Haven, Conn: Yale University Press.

Dwivedi, K., and Gupta, A. (2000). '"Keeping Cool": Anger Management through Group Work', *Support for Learning*, 15(2): 76–81.

Ellis, A. (1962). *Reason and Emotion in Psychotherapy*. New York: Lyle Stuart Press.

Ellsworth, P. C. (1994). 'Some Reasons to Expect Universal Antecedents of Emotion', in P. Ekman and R. J. Davidson (eds.), *The Nature of Emotion: Fundamental Questions* (pp. 150–54). New York: Oxford University Press.

Ellsworth, P. C., and Smith, C. A. (1988). 'From Appraisal to Emotion: Differences among Unpleasant Feelings', *Motivation and Emotion*, 12: 271–303.

Emery, R. E., Waldron, M., Katherine, M. K., and Aaron, J. (1999). 'Delinquent Behavior, Future Divorce or Nonmarital Childbearing, and Externalizing Behavior among Offspring: A 14-year Prospective Study', *Journal of Family Psychology*, 13(4): 568–79.

Eron, L. D. (1987). The Development of Aggressive Behavior from the Perspective of a Developing Behaviorism. *American Psychologist*, 42: 435–42.

Eastman, M., and Rozen, S. C. (1994). *Taming the Dragon in Your Child.* New York, NY: John Wiley and Sons, Inc.

Evans, G. W., Hygge, S., and Bullinger, M. (1995). 'Chronic Noise and Psychological Stress', *Psychological Science*, 6: 333–38.

Eysenck, S. B. J., and Eysenck, H. J. (1977). 'The Place of Impulsiveness in a Dimensional System of Personality', *British Journal of Social and Clinical Psychology*, 16: 57–68.

Fabes, R. A., and Eisenberg, N. (1992). 'Young Children's Coping with Interpersonal Anger', *Child Development*, 63(1): 116–28.

Farley, F. (1991). 'The Type-T Personality', in Lipsett, L. and Mitnick, L. (eds.), *Self-regulatory Behavior and Risk Taking: Causes and Consequences.* Norwood, N J: Ablex Pub.

Fergusson, D. M., Dimond, M. E., and Horwood, L. J. (1986). 'Childhood Family Placement History and Behaviour Problems in 6-year-old Children', *Journal of Child Psychiatry*, 27(2): 213–26.

Fivush, R. (1989). 'Exploring Differences in the Emotional Content of Mother-child Conversations about the Past', *Sex Roles*, 20: 675–91.

Frijda, N. H. (1986). *The Emotions.* New York, NY: Cambridge University Press.

Frijda, N. H., Kuipers, P., and Ster Chure, E. (1989). 'Relations among Emotion, Appraisal, and Emotional Action Readiness', *Journal of Personality and Social Psychology*, 57: 212–28.

Frodi, A. (1977). 'Sex Differences in the Perception of a Provocation: A Survey', *Perceptual and Motor Skills*, 44: 113–14.

Gelkopf, M. (1997). 'Laboratory Pain and Styles of Coping with Anger', *Journal of Psychology*, 131: 121–23.

Gjerde, P. F., Block, J., and Block, J. H. (1988). 'Depressive Symptoms and Personality During Late Adolescence: Gender Differences in the Externalization–Internalization of Symptom Expression', *Journal of Abnormal Psychology*, 97: 475–86.

Goldner, V., Penn, P., Scheinberg, M., and Walker, G. (1990). 'Love and Violence: Gender Paradoxes in Volatile Attachments', *Family Process*, 29(4): 343–64.

Goldstein, A. P., and Glick, B. (1987). 'Angry Youth—Reducing Aggression', *Corrections Today'*, 49: 38–42.

Goleman, D. (1995). *Emotional Intelligence.* New York: Bantam.

Gottman, J. M., Fainsilber-Katz, L., and Hooven, C. (1997). *Meta-emotion: How Families Communicate Emotionally.* Mahwah, NJ: Erlbaum.

Grier W. H., and P. M. Cobbs. (1968). *Black Rage.* New York: Harper Collins.

Grych, J. H., and Finchum, F. D. (1990). 'Marital Conflict and Children's Adjustment: A Cognitive-contextualist Framework', *Psychological Bulletin*, 108: 267–90.

Harburg, E., Julius, M., Kaciroti, N., Gleiberman, L., and Schork, M. A. (2003). 'Expressive/ Suppressive Anger-coping Responses, Gender, and Types of Mortality: A 17-year Follow-up (Tecumseh, Michigan, 1971–1988)', *Psychosomatic Medicine*, 65: 588–97.

Harty, S. C., Miller, C. J., Newcorn, J. H., and Halperin, J. M. (2009). 'Adolescent with Childhood ADHD and Comorbid Disruptive Behavior Disorder: Aggression, Anger and Hostility', *Child Psychiatry and Human Development*, 40(1), 85–97.

Halberstadt, A. G., and Eaton, K. L. (2003). 'A Meta-analysis of Family Expressiveness and Children's Emotion Expressiveness and Understanding', *Marriage and Family Review*, 34: 35–62.

Hegtvedt, K. A., and Markovsky, B. (1995). 'Justice and Injustice', in Karen S. Cook, Gary A. Fine, and James House (eds.), *Sociological Perspectives on Social Psychology*, pp. 257–80. Boston: Allyn Bacon.

Helmers, K. F., Baker, B., O'Kelly, B., and Tobe, S. (2000). 'Anger Expression, Gender, and Ambulatory Blood Pressure in Mild, Unmedicated Adults with Hypertension', *Annals of Behavioral Medicine*, 22: 60–64.

Herrald, M. M., and Tomaka, J. (2002). 'Patterns of Emotion-specific Appraisal, Coping, and Cardiovascular Reactivity During an Ongoing Emotional Episode', *Journal of Personality and Social Psychology*, 83: 434–50.

Hochschild, Arlie Russell and Anne Machung. (1989). *The Second Shift*. New York: Avon Books.

Hoglund, C. L., and Nicholas, K. B. (1995). 'Shame, Guilt, and Anger in College Students Exposed to Abusive Family Environments', *Journal of Family Violence*, 10: 141–57.

Howells, K., and Day, A. (2002). 'Grasping the Nettle: Treating and Rehabilitating the Violent Offender', *Australian Psychologist*, 37: 222–28.

Hughes, M. D., and Demo, D. H. (1989). 'Self-Perceptions of Black Americans: Self-Esteem and Personal Efficacy', *American Journal of Sociology*, 95: 132–59.

Hussong, A. M., and Chassin, L. (1994). 'The Stress-negative Affect Model of Adolescent Alcohol Use: Disaggregating Negative Affect', *Journal of Studies Alcohol*, 55: 707–18.

Izard, C. E. (1977). *Human Emotions*. New York: Plenum.

———. (1993). 'Organizational and Motivational Functions of Discrete Emotions', in M. Lewis and J. M. Haviland (eds.), *Handbook of Emotions* pp. 631–41. New York: Guilford.

Jacobs, G. A., Phelps, M., and Rohrs, B. (1989). 'Assessment of Anger Expression in Children: The Pediatric Anger Expression Scale', *Personality and Individual Differences*, 10(1): 59–65.

Jargowsky, P. A. (1994). 'Ghetto Poverty among Blacks in the 1980s', *Journal of Policy Management*, 13: 288–310.

Jenkins, J. M., Smith, M. A., and Graham, P. (1989). 'Coping with Parental Quarrels', *Journal of the American Academy of Child and Adolescent Psychiatry*, 28: 182–89.

Johnson, E. H. (1990). *The Deadly Emotions: The Role of Anger, Hostility, and Aggression in Health and Emotional Well-being*. New York: Praeger Publishers.

Joireman, J., Anderson, J., and Strathman, A. (2003). 'The Aggression Paradox: Understanding the Links among Aggression, Sensation Seeking, and the Consideration of Future Consequences', *Journal of Personality and Social Psychology*, 84: 1287–302.

Kassinove, H. (1995). *Anger Disorders: Definition, Diagnosis, and Treatment*. Washington, DC: Taylor and Francis.

Kaufman, G. (1996). *The Psychology of Shame: Theory and Treatment of Shame-based Syndromes* (2nd ed.). New York: Springer.

Kemper, T. D. (1987). 'How Many Emotions are There? Wedding the Social and the Autonomic Components', *American Journal of Sociology*, 93: 263–89.

Kerns, R. D., Rosenberg, R., and Jacob, M. C. (1994). 'Anger Expression and Chronic Pain', *Journal of Behavioral Medicine*, 17: 57–67.

Knox, S. S., Siegmund, K. D., Weidner, G., Ellison, R. C., Adelman, A., and Paton, C. (1998). 'Hostility, Social Support, and Coronary Heart Disease in the National Heart, Lung, and Blood Institute Family Heart Study', *American Journal of Cardiology*, 82: 1192–96.

Kollar, M., Groer, M., Thomas, S., and Cunningham, J. (1991). 'Adolescent Anger: A Developmental Study', *Journal of Child and Adolescent Psychiatric and Mental Health Nursing*, 4(1): 9–15.

Koss, M. P., Goodman, L. A., Browne, A., Fitzgerald, L. F., Keita, G. P., and Russo, N. F. (1994). *No Safe Haven: Male Violence against Women at Home, at Work, and in the Community*. Washington, D.C.: American Psychological Association.

Kring, A. M. (2000). 'Gender and Anger', in A. H. Fischer (ed.), *Gender and Emotion: Social Psychological Perspective* pp. 212–31. Cambridge: Cambridge University Press.

Kuebli, J., and Fivush, R. (1992). 'Gender Differences in Parent-Child Conversations about Past Emotions', *Sex Roles*, 27: 683–88.

Labouvie-Vief, G., Lumley, M. A., Jain, E., and Heinze, H. (2003). 'Age and Gender Differences in Cardiac Reactivity and Subjective Emotion Responses to Emotional Autobiographical Memories', *Emotion*, 3: 115–26.

Lane, S. D., and Cherek, D. R. (2000). 'Analysis of Risk Taking in Adults with a History of High Risk Behavior', *Drug and Alcohol Dependence*, 60(2): 179–87.

Larzelere, R. E. (2000). 'Child Outcomes of Non-abusive and Customary Physical Punish-Ment by Parents: An Updated Literature Review', *Clinical Child and Family Psychology Review*, 3: 199–221.

Leach, C. W., Iyer, A., and Pedersen, A. (2006). 'Anger and Guilt about In-group Advantage Explain the Willingness for Political Action', *Personality and Social Psychology Bulletin*, 32: 1232–45.

Leary, M. R., Twenge, J. M., and Quinlivan, E. (2006). 'Interpersonal Rejection as a Determinant of Anger and Aggression', *Personality and Social Psychology Review*, 10: 111–32.

Lewis, M. (1993). 'The Development of Anger and Rage', in R. A. Glick and S. P. Roofe (eds.), *Rage Power and Aggression: The Role of Affect in Motivation, Development, and Adaptation*, pp. 148–68. New Haven: Yale University Press.

Linden, W., Hogan, B. E., Rutledge, T., Chawla, A., Lenz, J. W., and Leung, D. (2003). 'There is More to Anger Coping Than "In" or "Out"', *Emotion*, 3: 12–29.

Lohr, J. M., and Bonge, D. (1982). 'The Factorial Validity of the Irrational Beliefs Test: A Psychometric Investigation', *Cognitive Therapy and Research*, 6: 225–30.

Lohr, J. M., Hamberger, L. K., and Bonge, D. (1988). 'The Relationship of Factorially Validated Measures of Anger-proneness and Irrational Beliefs', *Motivation and Emotion*, 12: 171–83.

Luhn, R. R. (1992). *Managing Anger: Methods for a Happier and Healthier Life.* United States of America: Crisp Publications, Inc.

Maccoby, E. E., and Martin, J. A. (1983). 'Socialization in the Context of the Family: Parent–Child Interaction', in P. Mussen (ed.) *Handbook of Child Psychology*, p. 4. New York: Wiley.

Mace, D. (1982). *Love and Anger in Marriage*, Grand Rapids, MI: Zondervan Publishing House of the Zondervan Corporation.

Mahon, N. E., Yarcheski, A., Yarcheski, T. J., and Hanks, M. M. (2006). 'Correlates of Low Frustration Tolerance in Young Adolescents', *Psychological Reports*, 99(1): 230.

McCann, B. S., and Matthews, K. A. (1988). 'Influences of Potential for Hostility, Type A Behavior, and Parental History of Hypertension on Adolescents' Cardiovascular Responses During Stress', *Psychophysiology*, 25: 503–11.

Miller, S. (1985). *The Shame Experience.* Hillsdale, NJ: Erlbaum

Mills, R. S., and Rubin, K. H. (1992). 'A Longitudinal Study of Maternal Beliefs about Children's Social Behaviors', *Merrill-Palmer Quarterly*, 38(4), 494–512.

Morris, T., Greer, S., Pettingale, K. W., and Watson, M. (1981). 'Patterns of Expression of Anger and their Psychological Correlates in Women with Breast Cancer', *Journal of Psychosomatic Research*, 25: 111–17.

Mueller, W. H., Grunbaum, J., and Labarthe, D. R. (2001). 'Anger Expression, Body Fat, and Blood Pressure in Adolescents: Project Heartbeat!', *American Journal of Human Biology*, 13: 531–38.

Murdoch, D., Pihl, R. O., and Ross, D. (1990). 'Alcohol and Crimes of Violence: Present Issues', *International Journal of Addictions*, 25: 1065–81.

Murphy, T., and Oberlin, L. H. (2001). *The Angry Child: Regaining Control When Your Child is Out of Control.* New York, NY: Clarkson Potter/Publisher.

Musante, L., Treiber, F., David, H., Waller, J., and Thompson, W. (1999). 'Assessment of Self-reported Anger Expression in Youth', *Assessment*, 6: 225–33.

Musher-Eizenman, D. R., Boxer, P., Danner, S., Dubow, E. F., Goldstein, S. E., and Heretick, D. M. L. (2004). 'Social Cognitive Mediators of the Relation of Environmental and Emotion Regulation Factors to Children's Aggression', *Aggressive Behavior*, 30, 389–408.

Namka, L. (1997). The Dynamics of Anger. Online document [http://members.aol.com/AngriesOut/teach6.htm].

Nelson, W. M., and Finch, A. J. (2000). *Children's Inventory of Anger (CHIA): Manual.* Los Angeles, CA: Western Psychological Service.

Novaco, R. W. (1986). 'Anger as a Clinical and Social Problem', in R. Blanchard and C. Blanchard (eds.), *Advances in the Study of Aggression* (pp. 1–67). New York, NY: Academic Press.

———. (2000). Anger. In A. E. Kazdin (Ed.), *Encyclopedia of Psychology.* Washington, D.C.: American Psychological Association and Oxford University Press.

———. (2003). *The Novaco Anger Scale and Provocation Inventory (NAS-PI).* Los Angeles: Western Psychological Services.

Novaco, R. W., Ramm, M., and Black, L. (2001). 'Anger Treatment with Offenders', in C. R. Hollin (ed.), *Handbook of Offender Assessment and Treatment* (pp. 281–296). Chichester, UK: Wiley and Sons Ltd.

Obstaz, M. (2008). 'Eight Types of Anger', Available online at http://www.angeresources.com (accessed on 20 June 2008).

Pearlin, L. I., and McKean, M. (1996). 'Stress and the Life-Course: A Paradigmatic Approach', *The Gerontologist*, 36(2): 239–50.

Penedo, F. J., Dahn, J. R., Kinsinger, D., Antoni, M. H., Molton, I., Gonzalez, J. S., Fletcher, M. A., Roos, B., Carver, C. S., and Schneiderman, N. (2006). 'Anger Suppression Mediates the Relationship between Optimism and Natural Killer Cell Cytotoxicity in Men Treated for Localized Prostate Cancer', *Journal of Psychosomatic Research*, 60(4): 423–27.

Piko, B. F., Keresztes, N., and Pluhar, Z. F. (2006). 'Aggressive Behavior and Psychosocial Health among Children', *Personality and Individual Differences*, 40: 885–95.

Pinhas, L., Toner, B. B., Ali, A., Garfinkel, P. E., and Stuckless, N. (1999). 'The Effects of the Ideal of Female Beauty on Mood and Body Satisfaction', *International Journal of Eating Disorders*, 25(2): 223–26.

Procter H. G., and R. Dallos. (2006). 'Making me Angry: The Constructions of Anger', in P. Cummins (ed.), *Working with Anger: A Constructivist Approach* (pp. 131–48). England: Wiley.

Raikkonen, K., Keskivaara, P., and Keltikangas-Jarvinen, L. (1992). 'Hostility and Social Support among Type A Individuals', *Psychology and Health*, 7: 289–99.

Ram, U. (2009). 'How Can We Reduce Anger', in Swati B. and Sunil S. (eds.), *The AHA-Syndrome and Cardiovascular Diseases* (pp. 44–55). New Delhi: Anamaya Publishers.

Ramsukhdas, Sw. (1996). *Srimad Bhagwadgita.* Gorakhpur: Gita Press.

Retzinger, S. M. (1987). 'Resentment and Laughter: Video Studies of the Shame–Rage Spiral', in H. B. Lewis (ed.), *The Role of Shame in Symptom Formation* (pp. 151–81). Hillsdale, NJ: Erlbaum.

Ricciardelli, L., and McCabe, M. (2001). 'Children's Body Image Concerns and Eating Disturbances: A Review of the Literature', *Clinical Psychology Review*, 21: 325–44.

Roseman, I. J., Spindel, M. S., and Jose, P. E. (1990). 'Appraisals of Emotion-eliciting Events: Testing a Theory of Discrete Emotions', *Journal of Personality and Social Psychology*, 59: 899–915.

Ross, D., and Roberts, P. (1999*). Income and Child Well-Being: A New Perspective on the Poverty Debate.* Ottawa: Canadian Council on Social Development.

Ross, C. E., and Van Willigen, M. (1996). 'Gender, Parenthood, and Anger', *Journal of Marriage and the Family*, 58: 572–84.

Rotton, J. and Frey, J. (1985). 'Air Pollution, Weather and Violent Crimes: Concomitant Time-series Analysis of Archival Data', *Journal of Personality and Social Psychology*, 49: 1207–20.

Saarni, C., and Buckley, M. (2002). 'Children's Understanding of Emotion Communication in Families', *Marriage and Family Review*, 34: 213–42.

Saini S., and Trama, S. (2006). 'Dating Violence'. *Bhave's Textbook of Adolescent Medicine* in S. Y. Bhave (ed.). New Delhi, India: Jaypee Brothers Medical Publishers (P) Ltd.

Saini, S. (2006a). 'Gender Differences in the Expression of Anger', *Asian Journal of Pediatric Practice*, 10(2): 9–13.

———. (2006b). 'Body Dissatisfaction and Psychological Problems', *Asian Journal of Pediatric Practice*, 10(1): 47–53.

———. (2009). 'Anger, Hostility and Aggression-The AHA-Syndrome', *The AHA-Syndrome and Cardiovascular Diseases* (pp. 1–15) in Swati B. and Sunil S. (eds.). New Delhi: Anamaya Publishers.

Saini, S., N., Goyal, and Sindhu. (2008). *Body Dissatisfaction and Psychological Problems among Adolescents,* Paper Presented at National Conference Organized by Department of Applied Psychology, Guru Jhambeshwar University of Science and Technology, Hisar, Haryana.

Salovey, P., and Mayer, J. D. (1990). 'Emotional Intelligence', *Imagination, Cognition, and Personality*, 9: 185–211.

Scherwitz, L., and Rugulies, R. (1992). 'Life-style and Hostility', in H. S. Friedman (ed.), *Hostility, Coping and Health* (pp. 77–98). Washington, DC: American Psychological Association.

Simons, R. L., Kuei-Hsiu Lin, L. C., Gordon, R. D. C. and Frederick O. L. (1999). 'Explaining the Higher Incidence of Adjustment Problems among Children of Divorce Compared with those in Two-parent Families', *Journal of Marriage and the Family*, 61: 1020–33.

Smith, T. W. (1992). 'Hostility and Health: Current Status of a Psychosomatic Hypothesis', *Health Psychology*, 11(3): 139–50.

Smith-Lovin, L. (1995). 'The Sociology of Affect and Emotion', in Karen S. Cook, Gary A. Fine, and James House (eds.), *Sociological Perspectives on Social Psychology*, pp. 118–48. Boston: Allyn Bacon.

Smith, D. C., Furlong, M., Bates, M., and Laughlin, J. D. (1998). 'Development of the Multidimensional School Anger Inventory for Males', *Psychology in the Schools*, 35(1): 1–15.

Snell, W. E., Jr., Gum, S., Shuck, R. L., Mosley, J. A., and Hite, T. L. (1995). 'The Clinical Anger Scale: Preliminary Reliability and Validity', *Journal of Clinical Psychology*, 2: 215–26.

Spielberger, C. D., Jacobs, G., Russell, S., and Crane, R. S. (1983). 'Assessment of Anger: The State-Trait Anger Scale', in J. N. Butcher and C. D. Spielberger (eds.), *Advances in Personality Assessment* (Vol. 2, pp. 161–89). Hillsdale, NJ: Lawrence Erlbaum.

Spielberger, C. D. (1999). *State-Trait Anger Expression Inventory*. Research Edition: Professional Manual. Florida: Psychological Assessment Resources.

Spielberger, C. D., Ritterband, L. M., Sydeman, S. J., Reheiser, E. C., and Unger, K. K. (1995). 'Assessment of Emotional States and Personality Traits: Measuring Psychological Vital Things', in N. J. Butcher (ed.), *Clinical Personality Assessment: Practical Approaches* (pp. 42–58). New York, NY: Oxford University Press.

Stevenson-Hinde, J. (1999). 'Individuals in Relationships', in R. Hinde, J. Stevenson-Hinde (eds.), *Relationships within Families: Mutual Influences* (pp. 68–82). Oxford (UK): Clarendon Press.

Stevenson, C. S., Whitmont, S., Bornholt, L., Livesey, D., and Stevenson, R. J. (2002). 'A Cognitive Remediation Programme for Adults with Attention Deficit Hyperactivity Disorder', *Australian and New Zealand Journal of Psychiatry*, 36(5): 610–16.

Steele, R. G., Elliott, V., and Phipps, S. (2003). 'Race and Health Status as Determinants of Anger Expression and Adaptive Style in Children', *Journal of Social and Clinical Psychology*, 22: 40–58.

Stice, E., and Whitenton, K. (2002). 'Risk Factors for Body Dissatisfaction in Adolescent Girls: A Longitudinal Investigation', *Developmental Psychology*, 38: 669–78.

Straus, M. A. (1993). *Ten Myths about Spanking Children*. Family Research Laboratory, University of New Hampshire.

Suinn, R. (2001). 'The terrible twos—Anger and Anxiety: Hazardous to Your Health', *American Psychologist*, 56: 27–36.

Tavris, C. (1982). *Anger*. New York: Simon and Schuster.

———. (1989). *Anger: The Misunderstood Emotion*. New York, NY: Simon and Schuster.

Taylor, J., and Novaco, R. W. (2005). *Anger Treatment for People with Developmental Disabilities*. Chichester: John Wiley and Sons.

Taylor, S. E., PePlau, L. A., and Sears, D. O. (1997). 'Aggression', in P. Janzow, P. Freund, B. Biller, and A. Roney (eds.), *Social Psychology* (9th ed., pp. 360–78). Upper Saddle River, NJ: Prentice Hall.

Thomas, S. P. (2002). 'Age Differences in Anger Frequency, Intensity, and Expression', *Journal of American Psychiatric Nurses Association*, 8: 44–50.

Thompson, R. A. (1994). 'Emotion Regulation: A Theme in Search of Definition', in N. A. Fox, (ed.), The Development of Emotion Regulation: Biological and Behavioral Considerations. *Monographs of the Society for Research in Child Development*, 59(2–3, Serial 240). Chicago, IL: The University of Chicago Press.

Tiedens, L. Z. (2001). 'Anger and Advancement versus Sadness and Subjugation: The Effect of Negative Emotion Expressions on Social Status Conferral', *Journal of Personality and Social Psychology*, 80, 86–94.

Trachtenberg, S., and Viken, R. J. (1994). 'Aggressive Boys in the Classroom: Biased Attributions or Shared Perceptions?', *Child Development*, 65: 829–35.

Trama, S., and Saini, S. (2005). 'Parenting and Children's Aggression-II', in M. Bhargava and S. Arora (eds.), (p. 278), *Parental Behavior* (2nd ed.). H. P. Bhargav Book House, Agra.

———. (2009). *Changing Scenario of Adolescent Aggression*. Paper Presented at National Seminar titled 'Adolescent Parenting: Recent Trends' Organized by Government College, Sector, 46B, Chandigarh, March 4.

Tsytsarev, S. V., and Grodnitzky, G. R. (1995). 'Anger and Criminality', in H. Kassinove (ed.), *Anger Disorders: Definitions, Diagnosis, and Treatment* (pp. 91–108). Washington, DC: Taylor & Francis.

Tucker-Ladd, C. (2006). Anger + Frustration. Retrieved online from http://www.thisisawar. com/DepressionAnger.htm dated (accessed on 20.04.2009).

Usha, R. (2009). 'How Can we Reduce Anger?', in Swati B. and Sunil S. (eds), *The AHA-Syndrome and Cardiovascular Diseases* (pp. 44–55). New Delhi: Anamaya Publishers.

Wang, X., Trivedi, R., Treiber, F., Snieder, H. (2005). 'Genetic and Environmental Influences on Anger Expression, John Henryism, and Stressful Life Events: The Georgia Cardiovascular Twin Study', *Psychosomatic Medicine* 67: 16–23.

Weiss, B., Dodge, K. A., Bates, J. E., and Petit, G. S. (1992). 'Some Consequences of Early Harsh Discipline: Child Aggression and a Maladaptive Social Information Processing Style', *Child Development*, 63: 1321–35.

Wiley, M. G., and Eskilson, A. (1982). 'Coping in the Corporation: Sex Role Constraints', *Journal of Applied Social Psychology*, 12: 1–11.

Wilkie, J. R., Myra M. F., and Kathryn, S. R. (1998). 'Gender and Fairness: Marital Satisfaction in Two-Earner Couples', *Journal of Marriage and the Family*, 60: 577–94.

Wood, K. C., Becker, J. A., and Thompson, J. K. (1996). 'Body Image Dissatisfaction in Preadolescent Children', *Journal of Applied Developmental Psychology*, 17: 85–100.

SECTION TWO

Various Effects of Anger on People

ANGER AND PHYSIOLOGICAL PROBLEMS

There are so many frustrations in our daily lives. People at home, school, offices, playground, and other public places are filled with anger and irritation, leading to loss of both physical and psychological health. In the present section, we are discussing physiological problems associated with anger and its associates hostility and aggression (The AHA-Syndrome) (Saini, 2009; Spielberger et al., 1995).

WHEN DOES ANGER OCCUR? (Anderson, 1978; Avrill, 1992; Horn and Towl, 1997; Kemper, 1987; Kassinove and Sukhodolsky, 1995; Novaco, 2000; Spielberger et al., 1985; Tavris, 1989)

- Anger is a normal reaction when circumstances are not fair or expectations are not met.
- It can be elicited by specific events, behaviors of self or others, and a combination of internal and external events.
- Anger is an individual's appraisal of an event or situation that mediates his/her emotional arousal and behavioural response, and it determines whether or not he/she is likely to feel angry and/or behave aggressively.
- Anger is likely to occur when a person believes their personal rights or codes have been violated. Similarly, anger can occur when a person feels powerless or threatened.

- When we do not get what we want at a particular moment, a flash of anger can come from within.
- Anger can also overwhelm us if we do not receive acceptance or recognition when we feel this is deserved.
- Anger also occurs when one blames oneself, circumstances, or faith (Ellsworth and Tong, 2006; Parkinson, 1999).

How Long Does Anger Last?

On an average, people report becoming angry two or three times per week (Averill, 1982). Someone who reports becoming angry every day or two to three times a day can be considered high in anger frequency (Novaco and Jarvis, 2002).

Anger Intensity Assessment can be Measured by

- Spielberger's (1999) State Trait Anger Expression Inventory (STAXI-2).
- Novaco's (2003) Anger Scale and Provocation Inventory (NAS-PI).

The normal experience of overt anger lasts only a few minutes. But the subtle forms of anger such as resentment, impatience, irritability, grouchiness, etc. can go on for hours and days at a time. Some people can carry a grudge for months or years or even a lifetime. The prolongation of anger arousal has several problematic consequences like high blood pressure and hypertension (Johnson, 1990).

Chronically Angry Persons

- Develop rigid styles of thinking, so they interpret others' words and deeds as hostile and automatically respond defensively.
- May feel the need to vent their hot temper physically by screaming, throwing things, or hitting.
- The main problem with such angry individuals is that they do not wish to change and tend to gravitate to those peers who are tolerant and reinforce their anger.

Such persons are very dangerous to self, family, society, and for the whole community.

WHAT HAPPENS TO YOUR BODY WHEN YOU GET ANGRY?

- When anger occurs, the body goes instantly into a series of mind–body reactions involving hormones, nervous system, and muscles.
- This involves a release of a hormone called adrenaline. Adrenaline increases the heart rate, respiratory rate, and raises the blood pressure also. There is shortness of breath, flushing of skin, muscle rigidity, and tightening in the jaw, stomach, shoulder, and hands.
- Increased blood flow enters the limbs and extremities in preparation for physical action. This is called the 'Fight or Flight' response (Raine, 1993).

Figure 2.1 Angry person

Someone who continues to dwell on anger experience may also be imagining violent retaliation.

WHAT HAPPENS TO OTHERS WHEN YOU GET ANGRY?

The behavioral consequences of your anger can also lead to burden for families and staff working in day and residential services, as well as to the wider community in the form of aggression and violence.

WHEN DOES ANGER LEAD TO AGGRESSION?

The tendency to express one's anger in an outwardly negative manner represents an outward directed style known as anger-out. Anger-out may involve the use of aggressive actions (e.g., assaultive behavior, destruction of property, or making offensive gestures) and/or aggressive verbal behavior (e.g., insults, offensive/inappropriate language, or shouting) (Spielberger et al., 1995). Anger drives both verbal and physical aggression. Verbal aggression pertains to threatening, abusive, and derogatory statements. Physical aggression produces physical harm or damage.

- When people get angry, their heart rate, blood pressure, and energy rises and hormone secretion increase (Kassinove and Trafrate, 2002).

- This physiological arousal is often expressed via aggression.
- Anger seems to facilitate psychological aggression in marital relationships (Saini, 2008).
- Aggression may include verbal attacks, threats, physical punishment, or restriction.

WHEN DOES ANGER CAUSE HOSTILITY? (SPIELBERGER ET AL., 1983)

Suppressed anger can facilitate hostility which is an attitude of disliking others and evaluating them negatively. Researchers have suggested that anger and hostility originate from family factors, such as attachment style and parental rearing behaviours (Grunbaum, Vernon, and Clasen, 1997).

THE AHA-SYNDROME

- The triad of anger, hostility, and aggression is collectively called 'The AHA-Syndrome' (Saini, 2009; Spielberger, 1999).
- This is often related to many physical (Lohr and Hamberger, 1990) and psychological problems (Tafrate et al., 2002).
- The prolonged levels of anger results in many other problems like high blood pressure, hypertension, stroke, cancer, arthritis, circulatory diseases, obesity, cancer, gastrointestinal diseases, pain, headaches, stomach aches, skin rashes (Knox et al., 1998; Scherwitz and Rugulies, 1992; Thomas et al., 2000).

WHAT IS THE PHYSIOLOGICAL PROGRESSION OF ANGER?

- Each negative emotion is associated with a unique pattern of physiological, hormonal, and neurohormonal changes in our body. These constitute a bridge that links negative emotions with disease processes, causing specific diseases in the body. Thus, anger is uniquely associated with exceedingly high levels of both systolic (signified by the upper number) and diastolic (signified by the lower number) blood pressure reactivity and thus anger causes high blood pressure

(Smith and Allred, 1989). So people who get angry often land up with chronic hypertension.

- Anger also causes damage to the coronary arteries, and can result in transient deficiencies of blood supply to the heart (ischemia), and ultimately in a heart attack (MI). So angry people are more prone to chest pain and coronary disease and death. Suppressed anger has well-established links to elevated physiological arousal and sustained hypertension (Robins and Novaco, 2000).

IN WHICH PART OF THE BRAIN IS ANGER GENERATED?

- Emotions are generated within the two almond-shaped structures in the brain called the amygdala. The amygdala is responsible for identifying threats and reacting accordingly to initiate action within the body (Adolphs et al., 1999).
- The amygdala gives instant response hence the reactions are initiated before the cortex (section of the brain responsible for thought and judgment) is able to ascertain the logic and reasonability of the reaction (Peveler and Johnston, 2002).
- Hence anger is impulsive and occurs before the rational part of the brain takes a decision. Hence it becomes important to train the mind to control anger as we often make hasty and rash decisions in anger which we later regret but often it is too late.
- Inside the brain also neurotransmitter chemicals known as catecholamines are released, causing an increase in energy that generally lasts up to several minutes. This triggers a lasting state of arousal.
- Some researchers have argued that impulsive anger and aggression arise as a consequence of faulty emotion regulation (Davidson et al., 2000).

HOSTILITY

'Hostility is an attitude that involves disliking others and evaluating them negatively.' Hostile people are often described as being stubborn, impatient, hotheaded, and having a cynical attitude. They frequently engage in arguments and may verbally state that they feel like hitting something or someone. Hostility often evokes peer rejection (Dodge, 1991) and reciprocal hostile mood from others (Karasawa, 2003).

- A hostile person is the one who
  - immediately gets angry when he has to wait in traffic or when confronted with a long line at the grocery checkout;
  - is constantly yelling at his loved ones;
  - often experience rejection from their roommates (Hokanson and Butler, 1992).

If you are behaving in such a way remember you may be slowly killing yourself.

People in today's society have a growing disrespect for others because of negative thoughts. These negative thoughts lead to hostile behavior in different areas of life.

- Anger and hostility are associated with many sources of physical and psychological distress (Kassinove and Tafrate, 2002), e.g., people who remain angry and hostile much of the time have less physical activity, less self-care, more smoking, more alcohol consumption, and more frequent drinking and driving (Calhoun et al., 2001).
- A negative emotional state makes aggressive children more prone to attribute hostile intentions to other, making the children behave even more aggressively (Dodge, 1985).

Anger and hostility are significant risk factors for diseases like coronary heart disease, asthma, diabetes, and other psychological distress. If you have a coronary heart disease, remember when you get angry you are evoking physiological responses that are potentially life threatening. Very often anger precipitates an attack or death. In people with coronary disease those with high levels of anger have

Figure 2.2 Don't be angry all the time

- 3 times increased risk of premature coronary vascular disease,
- 3.5 times higher risk of premature coronary heart disease, and
- 6.4 times higher risk of premature heart attack, i.e., MI (Myocardial Infarct) (Chang et al., 2002).

LEARN TO 'LET GO' OF YOUR ANGER

- Some angry individuals keep thinking over the frustration/harassment situation, this is called rumination and this preservative thinking to anger can cause an increase in negative effect e.g., anger or anxiety (Brosschot and Thayer, 2004). This causes prolonged higher cardiovascular activation, making them more prone to heart attack.
- Chronic anger also has increased rates of testosterone production and platelet formation, which cause coronary artery disease (Siegman, 1994).

ANGER AND PHYSICAL HEALTH

HYPERTENSION

Whether you hold your anger inside you or frequently express it, you can be causing damage to your physical health.

- Anger held inward is implicated in the etiology and maintenance of essential hypertension (Diamond, 1982; Johnson, 1984).
- High scores on Spielberger's STAXI-2, Anger-in scale, a trait measure of anger suppression, were associated with higher blood pressure levels (Sul et al., 1995).
- Persons who show a 'high outward expression of anger' have exaggerated diastolic blood pressure response, in contrast to those who 'hold their anger in' (Suchday and Larkin, 2001).
- Defensiveness during anger episodes causes high diastolic blood pressure (Pauls and Stemmler, 2003).
- High anger-out person exhibits biases in their appraisals of situations, blaming others for bad events and judging that the negative behavior was intentional (Hazebroek et al., 2001).

Figure 2.3 Anger and high blood pressure

CARDIOVASCULAR HEART DISEASES

Cardiovascular diseases are a leading cause of death and disability around the world. Most of the risk factors are associated with unhealthy lifestyle factors such as smoking, obesity, and inadequate exercise, lack of social support, various emotional disorders, and prolonged stressors. However, there is also a very strong relationship between angry temperament, high blood pressure, and cardiovascular heart diseases. Clinical evidence indicates that anger evokes physiological responses that are potentially life-threatening in individuals with coronary artery disease. In addition, emotional stress, anger, and worry have a profound influence on the severity, frequency, and treatment responsiveness in coronary artery disease (Futterman and Lemberg, 2002).

Symptoms of coronary artery disease can be triggered by various psychological factors such as anger, hostility, aggression, mental stress, and depression (Harburg et al., 2003; Rosenberg et al., 2001; Saini, 2009).

STROKE OR PARALYSIS ATTACK

Anger expression also has a strong relationship with the risk of getting stroke. Men who are always angry are at twice the risk of stroke (Everson et al., 1999) compared with men who are less angry, even with the same parameters of age, resting blood pressure, smoking, alcohol consumption, body mass index, cholesterol, and socioeconomic status. Outwardly expressed anger has greater than 6-fold increased risk of stroke, low level of anger expression has nearly half the risk of nonfatal heart attacks and a significant reduction in the risk of stroke compared to men with moderate levels of anger expression (Patricia, 2003).

LUNG DISEASE AND ASTHMA

- Asthma is not a psychological condition but emotions like anger, fear, crying, excitement, have a significant impact in triggering asthmatic symptom in people who already have asthma.

Figure 2.4   Asthma and anger

- Anger particularly trait anger is a significant risk factor in asthma disease (Friedman and Booth-Kewley, 1987; Wright et al., 1998).
- Older men who have anger and hostility lose lung power faster than is expected in normal aging (Kubzansky et al., 2006).
- Negative emotions cause problems with pulmonary function in people with respiratory diseases such as asthma and chronic obstructive pulmonary disease (Steptoe, 1984).

DIABETES

Diabetes is one of the major healthcare problems in almost every society around the world. It involves abnormalities in the production and/or utilization of the pancreatic hormone, insulin, which is essential for glucose metabolism.

The primary diagnostic criterion for diabetes includes presence of abnormally high levels of glucose in the bloodstream, also known as hyperglycemia.

- Persons who have higher anger temperament subscale scores have a slightly increased risk of Type 2 diabetes and obesity (Golden et al., 2006).
- Persons with depression, hostility, and anger have abnormal glucose and insulin, especially women who are at an increasing risk of Type 2 diabetes and cardiovascular disease (Suarez, 2006).

CANCER

Cancer involves the uncontrolled growth of abnormal cells that have mutated from normal tissues. This growth can kill when these cells prevent normal function of vital organs or spread throughout the body, damaging essential systems.

- There is a relationship between several psychological factors that lead to impairment of endocrine and immune functions, which may predispose an individual to the development of cancer (Garssen and Goodkin, 2001; Harburg et al., 2003; Thomas et al., 2000).
- Anger can be a precursor to development of cancer. Suppressed anger is a psychological risk factor for the development of cancer, and also a factor in its progression after diagnosis (Thomas et al., 2000).

- In one study, anger was the only attribute, which successfully distinguished between benign and malignant breast disease (Morris et al., 1981). Other studies have shown that many women have developed breast cancer after a painful divorce or death of a husband. The repression/suppression of negative emotions has long been considered detrimental for breast cancer patients, leading to poor coping, progression of symptoms, and general lower quality of life (Lieberman and Goldstein, 2005).

Expressing your anger and coming to terms with your cancer is helpful. Patients with cancer who were able to express anger and other emotions had more cancer-killing lymphocytes at their tumor sites. The patients who openly expressed their anger lived longer than those who expressed little or no anger (Temoshok and Dreher, 1992). Thus, one of the main characteristics of a personality (called Type C personality) prone to cancer is either the repression or the inability to express or feel anger.

ARTHRITIS

Arthritis is caused by inflammation of the tissue lining the joints. The common signs of inflammation are redness, swelling, heat, and pain. The two most common type of arthritis are osteoarthritis and rheumatoid.

Anger can be one of the causes of persistent arthritis. Anger and frustration increases the intensity and duration of pain in patients of arthiritis (Gaskin et al., 1992).

Figure 2.5   Arthritis and pain

OBESITY

Obesity is a condition characterized by increased body weight caused by excessive accumulation of fat.

Figure 2.6   Overeating and Obesity

- Anger experience and expression are the common causes of obesity. Adolescents who cannot manage their anger often have weight problems. The angry person continues to swallow his/her anger with every mouthful of food. Study has shown that teenagers who lose their temper or squash feelings of anger are more likely to be overweight than other teens (Mueller et al., 2001).
- Body fat or body mass is often associated with unhealthy forms of anger expression in adolescents (Mueller et al., 2001).
- Anger management may be an important component in treatment of obesity (Edman et al., 2005).

IRRITABLE BOWEL SYNDROME (IBS)

- It is the most commonly diagnosed functional digestive (or gastrointestinal) disorder. Various lifestyle, physical, environmental, and psychological factors have been implicated in the development and maintenance of IBS.
- Both psychological and physical dysfunctions affect the functioning of the digestive system (Drossman, 1999). Patients respond to emotional and environmental stimulation with increased colon motor activity (Whitehead et al., 1980).
- Anger may have a significant although different effect on gastric motor activity in IBS patients compared to normal subjects (Welgan and Meshkinpour, 2000).
- Hyperactivity of the stomach (i.e., engorgement of the mucus linings of the stomach and intestines, increased muscular contractions of the intestinal wall, and accelerated secretion of certain neuroendocrines, accompanies aggressive feelings, anger, and resentment; while fear has an inhibitory effect (Baldaro et al., 1996).

Figure 2.7   Pain

PAIN

Pain is a complex phenomenon that has both emotional and physical components.

- Emotions like anger, threat, fear, hostility, depression, are the major psychological factors that play a huge role in the experience of pain.
- Unexpressed anger can be converted into pain (Breuer and Freud, 1956; Engel, 1959; Merskey and Spear, 1967).
- Unexpressed anger can increase the unpleasantness of pain experience (Pilowsky, 1986).
- In chronic pain patients, the style of inhibiting the expression of angry feelings was the strongest predictor of pain intensity and pain behavior (Kerns et al., 2005).
- Anger and frustration can increase the intensity and duration of pain in patients with various diseases like low back pain, various muscle, and nerve pains like myofascial pain, causalgia (Wade et al., 1990), arthritis, and fibromyalgia (Gaskin et al., 1992).
- High levels of anger were related to greater perceived pain in individuals with spinal cord injuries (Summers et al., 1991).
- Anger-out was significantly and positively associated with chronic pain intensity in war veterans. They have chronic back pain and pain in multiple body sites (Lombardo et al., 2005).

HEADACHE

Figure 2.8   Headache

Negative emotional state like anger and depression can cause headaches and other body pains. Patients with headache suppress their anger more than people without headache even after taking into account factors like depression, anxiety, and trait-anger (Nicholson et al., 2003).

- Patients with migraine and tension headache have high scores on anger suppression scale (anger-in) which are significantly higher than patients with tension headache (Hatch et al., 2005).
- Depression is seen significantly related with the anger-in score in all the patients (Venable et al., 2001).

- Patients with migraine experience anxiety and/or guilt after expressing anger and are more inhibited in expressing angry feelings than people who do not suffer from chronic headache (Bihldorff et al., 1971).
- Patients with migraine showed more intensity and frequency of headaches if they are angry and have higher anger-out scores (Materazzo et al., 2000).
- In posttraumatic headache, patients' greater anger-out was associated with greater headache-related disability and is specially associated with depression (Duckro et al., 1995).

OTHER HEALTH EFFECTS

Anger expression and suppression has been related to several biochemical and molecular markers, which are relevant for key diseases processes.

- High levels of anger have been related directly to elevated cortisol secretion i.e., the stress related hormone during normal daily activities (van Eck et al., 1996).
- High levels of anger show higher triglyceride reactivity, relative to those with a more flexible style of anger expression (Davidson et al., 1999).
- Impulsive anger-out heightens glucose levels and a more negative lipid profile of high total serum cholesterol, low density lipoproteins, and triglyceride levels, as well as heightened glucose levels (Siegman et al., 2002).

SUMMARY

Anger is a normal human emotion, sometimes necessary, but if not controlled leads to many serious health consequences. Problems like cardiovascular heart diseases, hypertension, obesity, cancer, are the leading causes of deaths around the world. Empirical findings have shown that anger expression, anger-in, anger-out, anger coping styles are the important risk factors in the etiology of these major illnesses. Many researches have shown that anger management has profound effect in reducing symptoms of health illnesses. Anger is the most poorly addressed emotion; keeping this in mind, important anger management techniques for laymen to self-control this devastating emotion have been discussed in the next section of the book.

ANGER AND PSYCHOLOGICAL PROBLEMS

Emotions play a very significant role in daily life of an individual's experience of self and orientation toward others. Anger is a complex emotion and is normal in everyday life—experienced at home, office, and public places. Anger is composed of interrelated elements and affects other emotions and psychological problems, leading to more serious problems.

Figure 2.9   Anger leads to more serious problems

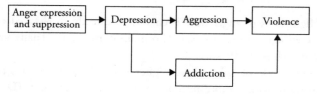

DEPRESSION

Anger is a strong accompaniment to depression (Kim and Park, 2002). Depressed individual have more anger attacks, which is further associated with more depressed symptoms.

- Depression and anger lead to serious health problems. Even those who recover from depression, as compared to never depressed people, show higher levels of anger suppression and fear of anger expression (Brody et al., 1999).
- Anger attacks among pregnant and 18-months postpartum women have been reported to be more. It is often associated with depression, directed at their spouses and/or children and being related to lower satisfaction with social support (Mammen et al., 1999).
- It has been noted that children with anger problems are four times more likely to experience a depressive episode in young adulthood (Mason et al., 2004).

- Increased levels of anger suppression are associated with less improvement in depression (Burns et al., 1998).
- People who are introvert and suppress their feeling of anger are more likely to be hostile and depressed (Burns et al., 1998).
- When anger is not regulated properly it often turns to depression (Spielberger et al., 1995).
- Hopelessness, which is a central cognitive component of depression, is known to be correlated with the explosive expression of anger (Kashani et al., 1997).
- Depressive disorder patients have significantly higher anger-out scores on the Spielberger anger expression measure (Koh et al., 2002) and patients with major depression were twice as likely to report anger attacks as patients with panic disorder (Gould et al., 1996).

PSYCHIATRIC DISORDERS

Patients with psychiatric and psychological problems often have a lot of anger. Patients with panic disorder, obsessive-compulsive disorder, and social phobia have a significantly greater propensity to experience anger than controls. Patients with panic disorder also have significantly greater levels of anger aggression (Moscovitch et al., 2007).

EATING DISORDERS

- Eating disorders are most common among female adolescents and young women. Pressure from family, peer group, media, and society to be thin results in low self-esteem, depression, and impulsivity among them; these are the common causes for eating disorders.
- Research has indicated that feelings of depression and high levels of negative affect lead to disordered eating (Stice, 2001; Wertheim et al., 2001).

There are two types of eating disorders—anorexia nervosa and bulimia nervosa.

- Anorexia nervosa is a condition characterized by an inadequate and unhealthy pattern of eating and an excessive concern to control body weight and shape.

- Bulimia nervosa is a serious, potentially life-threatening eating disorder characterized by overeating (binging) and then purging to get rid of the calories consumed.

Eating disorders are due to serious emotional and physical problems, mostly seen in adolescents and women. Internalized anger and anger suppression are important factors in the etiology of eating disorders. Anger and aggression increase the complexity of the clinical features, change the prognosis, and cause a more difficult management of eating disorder.

- Seventy-five percent of overeating is caused by emotions. People usually eat large quantities of food in response to feelings, and not to hunger.
- Anger discomfort can cause disordered eating for males and females. Anger management is an important component in treatment for obese young adults (Edman et al., 2005).
- Women with eating disorders have higher levels of anger and anger suppression, particularly if the diagnosis included bulimic symptoms. Different aspects of anger were associated with specific bulimic behaviors (Waller et al., 2003).

Figure 2.10 Eating disorder: A young girl denying to eat food

Figure 2.11 Body dissatisfaction

Body dissatisfaction arises from negative evaluation of one's figure and body parts. Adolescents are increasingly surrounded with media images of perfect body in advertisements, on television, and in movies. In almost every society, being thin is highly valued among women, whereas being slim and muscular is strongly appreciated among men.

Negative affect is a potential risk factor in developing body dissatisfaction. Negative mood associated with depression may develop feeling of inadequacy and discrepancy in actual body image and ideal body parts. Experimental studies have found that acute negative affect inductions resulting in acute body dissatisfaction in girls (Baker et al.,1995; Taylor and Cooper, 1992). Adolescents who feel angry, lonely, and socially anxious due to their poor body image, develop more body dissatisfaction (Saini, 2006).

STRESS

Anger expression is related to high levels of stress (Tavris, 1989). They are like identical twins. If anger rises, stress rises and if anger falls, stress falls. Stress is accumulated in the mind over a period of time, while anger is a spontaneous overflow of powerful ill feelings. Workers who are more stressed feel less competent when compared with workers who experience less stress (Bhagat and Allie, 1989), make fewer rational decisions (Keinan, 1987), and want to quit their jobs (Chen and Spector, 1992), and hence the feeling of frustration, anger, and aggression.

- Persons who are high in dispositional anger experience greater stress in their environments and tend to cope with it more poorly. Such individuals not just respond to highly stressful situation with greater reactivity but also create more stressful situations for them (Jamner et al., 1991). There is evidence that susceptibility to anger affect individuals, which involves difficulty in understanding and relating to other people, thereby contributing to increased stress on the job (ibid.).
- Stress is also related to absenteeism, lack of productivity, and decreased turnover (Jackson, 1983), and can lead to the acts of sabotage, interpersonal aggression, hostility, poor health, and even injury (Chen and Spector, 1992).
- Exposure to nature such as trees, grass, and flowers can effectively reduce stress (Ulrich et al., 1991).

FEELING OF BEING CONSTANTLY UNDER THREAT

Anger is aroused when threat is detected, malevolence is inferred, and approach or attack motivation is gauged. Persons with high anger dispositions are highly vigilant in sensing threat and quick in response. They unnecessarily perceive threat from others and end up in fights and violence. Angry people often believe that they have been threatened or harmed and justification for harming the transgressor is built in (DiGiuseppe and Tafrate, 2006).

- Threat sensing is confirmation biased and the anger responses are highly automatized. The strong arousal overrides inhibitory controls of aggressive behavior, and the threat-anger-aggression responses forge a positive feedback loop.

   More the perception of threat, more the anger and aggression and conversely, more the anger and aggression, greater the readiness to perceive threat and the likelihood of new inputs that will constitute threat.
- Belief in the ability to cope with a potential threat also causes anger (Frijda, 1986).

SUICIDAL IDEATION

Anger, hostility, and aggression are the common problems of adolescents in almost every society. Adolescents with hostile behavior pattern and angry temperament are likely to engage in risky behaviors and have suicidal ideation (Saini, 2007).

- Maladaptive expression of anger has been linked to suicidal ideation and suicide attempts by adolescents (Boergers et al., 1998; Goldston et al., 1996).
- Adolescents who are depressed are at greater risk of attempting suicide if they also manifest high levels of anger and aggression (Stein et al., 1998, Prigerson and Slimack, 1999).

Figure 2.12   Suicidal ideation

ANGER AND BEHAVIORAL PROBLEMS

Everyday life is filled with conflicts in all walks of life e.g., at the family level, between parents, children, husband and wife; at the school level, between teachers and students, among teachers and among students; at the society level, among different groups on various issues such as caste, religion, etc., both at national and international levels. Studies have been done and are ongoing to unfold the root cause of these increasing conflicts in our society. It has been found that negative emotions are the major factors behind all these disturbances. Anger is one such negative emotion, which is very significant in causing all these conflicts. In the following section, we are emphasizing on behavioral influences of anger.

AGGRESSION

Anger leads to aggression that can take many forms.

Sexual aggression

Sexual aggression is any kind of sexual activity against a person's will. Most of the crimes relating to youth are linked in some way to sexual aggression. Generally, it is found that such instances are found due to anger in known relationships because of many reasons.

- Exposure to sexually stimulating materials may elicit aggressive behavior in youth who are predisposed to aggression.
- Researches have shown that sexual aggression is motivated by anger rather than by sexuality (Bianchi, 1976; Briere and Malamuth, 1983; Sigelrnan et al., 1984). These also noted an association between sexual and physical aggression in college-going men.

Sports aggression

Fights, threats, verbal abuse, indecent gestures, and other violent actions are the common characteristics of today's sport. Anger and hostility are the common factors behind such behaviors (Saini and Bhave, 2008). Nowadays, competition in sports has shown to increase frustration that leads to increased predisposition for violent actions by both players and spectators.

Workplace aggression

Workplace aggression and violence are increasing day by day in all organizations. Anger is one of the most frequently experienced emotions and the cause of frustration and aggression at workplace. Anger episodes at work may affect the quality of job satisfaction, team interactions, performance, perceptions of injustice, deviance, dissatisfaction, revenge, and incivility (Barsade, 2002; Boccialetti, 1988; Glomb, 2002; Andersson and Pearson, 1999; Bies et al., 1997; Spector, 1997).

- These anger experiences are triggered by a number of events such as perceived personal attacks, unfair treatment, job stress, workload, perceived incivility, harassment.

Figure 2.13 Workplace aggression

- Employees frequently report being the targets of aggression including different forms of verbal harm such as talking behind others' backs and interrupting others while speaking; the least frequent are forms of overt physical aggression such as physical assault and attack with a weapon.
- Angry behavior may evoke negative response from coworkers. This mistrust of others may impair job performance (Buss, 1987).
- Anger experience at workplace is associated with many health concerns, including hypertension and cardiovascular heart diseases (Schnall et al., 1998).
- Workplace anger also has negative outcomes for the organization leading to theft, revenge, and even violence and aggression (Deffenbacher et al., 1996).
- According to a leading conflict management practitioner in America, workplace anger creates a 'pressure-cooker environment that can lead to hostility and even violence' (Daniels cited in Maurice, 1999).

DATING VIOLENCE

- Romantic relationship is an important aspect of adolescence. Individuals during their adolescence are involved in a variety of romantic relationships, including dating, feelings of tenderness, and love.

- The other sex is a frequent source of strong emotions. The majority of these emotions are positive but a substantial proportion is negative also. When people do not get the desired response they get angry, depressed, and violent.

Figure 2.14 Dating violence

(a)

(b)

- Dating violence is a pattern of violent behavior that someone uses against a girlfriend/boyfriend. More than 25 percent of adolescents are victims of dating violence or aggression (Wolfe and Feiring, 2000). There are so many cases reported in daily newspapers, magazines, and other media of dating violence including slapping, kicking, tearing hair, pushing–pulling, hitting, attempted rape, rape, date rape, group rape, drug abuse, aggression, and even murder. Young girls are most vulnerable to this.

- Negative emotions are found to be at the core of dating violence. Eighty-nine percent of teenagers between the ages of 13 and 18 yrs have been in relationships and 9–46 percent of high school students are involved in dating violence. Nearly 80 percent of those who have been physically abused on dating continue to date their abusers (Watson et al., 2001).

- Romantic relational aggression has strong relationship with relational victimization in romantic relationship and are associated with loneliness, depression, peer rejection, social anxiety, and alcohol abuse (Crick and Grotpeter, 1995; Bagner et al., 2007; Saini, 2008).

MARITAL CONFLICT AND DOMESTIC VIOLENCE

Marriage is said to be a social contact between two members of opposite sex where both members pledge to live together, share their moments of love, joys, and sorrows, etc. When certain wishes and dreams about marriage are not met, marital conflicts arise.

Figure 2.15   Marital discord and anger

- Criticism and resentment tend to be expressed in angry, hostile, and irritating ways. Most married people initially try to build a smooth, close, and safe relationship, preferably one without friction. In this process, sometimes the roles for a husband and wife become very rigidly defined; there is no freedom, no room for growth or change.

Figure 2.16   Marital conflict

- Sometimes, people think they need to pretend to be or feel in a certain way to appeal to their spouse. These little dishonesties in intimate moments are practised when your spouse may not accept you as you are.
- Arguments about money, recognition, and attention are the other factors which result in conflicts between husbands and wives. These result in everyday quarrels and affect both partners.
- A male's anger arises out of insecure attachment (Dutton, 1999). Insecure people become angry and are unable to maintain a loving relationship. Research has shown that secure attachment is related to lower proneness to anger, more constructive anger goals, more adaptive response, and more positive affect in anger episodes (Mikulincer, 1998).

- Anger and hostility are the root causes of today's marital conflicts and break ups. Hostility is associated with an increased risk for exposure to marital difficulties in the future (Miller et al., 1995; Newton and Kiecolt-Glasser, 1995).Therefore, anger management tactics are suggested for living a better married life.
- Anger and hostility often end up in domestic violence.
- Psychological aggression (i.e., acts of recurring criticism toward a partner, acts of isolation and domination of a partner, destroying partner's belongings, malicious name calling, etc.) in marital relationships is also on the rise. Psychological aggression is also related with interparental physical aggression, parent-to-child physical aggression, and angry feelings toward relationship partner (Taft et al., 2006; Saini et al., 2008).
- Furthermore, marital conflict has been shown to invoke fear, anger, aggression, depression, and delinquency in children (Cummimgs, 1987) (Scheier and Botvin, 1997).

DRIVING AGGRESSION

Traffic accidents are increasing day-by-day and are the leading cause of deaths around the world especially in India where youth population and motor vehicles are increasing daily. Research has shown that most of these accidents are due to inappropriate behavior of the drivers instead of technical failure.

- Anger is the root cause of aggressive driving among adolescents. Everyday anger expression has a positive relationship with aggressive driving.
- The common risky driving behaviors are speeding, tailgating, following too closely, gesturing, yelling, improper passing, sustained horn honking, flashing headlights, flashing high beams, jumping red lights, jumping stop signs, overtaking, and preventing other drivers from passing, etc. (Saini, 2008b).

Figure 2.17 Driving aggression

- In driving simulations, high-anger drivers were twice as likely to become involved in an accident, while under a high stress situation (Deffenbacher et al., 2003).
- Anger was the only mood state associated with speeding in adolescents (Arnett et al., 1997).
- Reckless driving was associated with elevated state of anger in college students (Morris et al., 1996).
- Individuals who reported high levels of anger were also more likely to be outwardly aggressive while driving than they were in non-driving situations (Lawton and Nutter, 2002).

AGGRESSIVE PERSONALITY

Anger plays an important role in the making of an aggressive personality. Anger reduces inhibitions against aggression in the following ways (Berkowitz, 2001).

Figure 2.18 Aggressive personality

First, it provides a justification for an aggressive retaliation. It can interfere with higher-level cognitive process that is normally used in moral reasoning and judgment.

Second, anger allows a person to maintain an aggressive intention over time. Anger increases attention to the provoking events, increases the depth of processing of those events, and therefore improves recall of these events. Thus, anger allows the person to reinstate the state that was present in originally provoking situation, which means a person is chronically angry over a situation that is long over.

Third, anger is used as an information cue. It informs people about causes, faults, and possible ways of responding (e.g., retaliation). If anger is triggered in an ambiguous social situation, the anger experience itself helps resolve the ambiguities.

Fourth, anger primes aggressive thoughts, scripts, and associated expressive motor behaviors. These anger-related knowledge structures are used to interpret the situation and to provide aggressive responses to the situation.

Fifth, anger energizes behavior by increasing arousal levels.

ALCOHOL AND DRUG ABUSE

Alcohol consumption is one of the most prevalent health risk factors among adolescents. Alcohol and drug abuse have also been found to be contributing to sexually transmitted diseases like HIV/AIDS, and even to rapes, violence, and teenage pregnancy.

Figure 2.19　Alcohol addiction

- Anger, particularly trait anger is highly associated with smoking, alcohol, and drug abuse behavior.
- In youth, elevated levels of anger and irritability predispose them to subsequent use of alcohol and drugs (Tarter et al., 1995).
- It has been found that in most traffic accidents alcohol was the main cause of angry arguments.
- Women with a anger problem are more prone to smoking, caffeine use, and alcohol consumption (Calhoun et al., 2001).
- Improper health maintenance behavior is associated with high anger experience, expression, and hostility (Johnson-Saylor, 1991).

SENSATION SEEKING BEHAVIOR

Sensation seeking is a powerful and indispensable component of our lives such that if we don't take our sensation seeking desires in a controlled way, there are chances of developing many addictions and risky behaviors that can result in a great loss to ourselves and society as a whole. Sensation seeking may be defined as 'the need for varied, novel, and complex sensations and experiences, and the willingness to take physical, financial, and social risks for the sake of such experiences' (Zuckerman, 1979).

Anger is a significant risk factor in sensation seeking behavior (Joireman et al., 2003). People who have negative emotions seek novelty in their behavior or to remove boredom, engage in many risky behaviors. Angry people often enjoy sensation in high speed, tailgating, horn honking, jumping red lights, etc., and the outcomes are disability and death. Such characteristics are commonly found in young children.

Sensation seeking individuals tend to engage in behaviors that increase the amount of stimulation they experience. Studies have been conducted which list association between sensation seeking and maladaptive behaviors like alcohol abuse, smoking, drug abuse, risky driving, multiple sexual partner, high risk sports, internet addiction, which in turn have a strong relation with anger, hostility, physical and verbal aggression, among other antisocial behaviors.

- When sensational experiences are lacking, some people get into a state of madness and can indulge in various thrill-seeking and aggressive acts.
- When sensation seeking desires are not met, some people feel bored, anxious, and depressed and they may develop habits of drinking, drug abuse (cocaine, heroin, etc.) gambling, aggressive driving, and unprotected sex leading to HIV risk, thereby putting themselves and others at greater risks.
- Sensation seekers are generally less affiliative, less socialized, and lower in self-control. They are less satisfied in their relationships and more inclined toward risky behaviors (Zuckerman, 1979).

IMPULSIVE BEHAVIOR

Impulsivity is acting out on the spur of the moment without thinking the outcome of the behavior. Impulsive people are inclined to act on impulse rather than thought. They cannot resist their impulses. Studies have highlighted the strong relationships among impulsivity, anger, and aggression (Joireman et al., 2003; Saini 2009a).

- Adolescents have poor control on their impulses and are inclined to act on impulse rather than thought. People with a tendency to 'lose their temper easily' possess high levels of both impulsivity and anger (Barratt, 1985).
- Accident repeaters have poor control of hostile impulses and have anti-social tendencies (Novaco, 1991).
- Impulsivity is related with smoking, and alcohol and substance abuse (Baker et al., 2003; Patton, et al., 1995).
- It has been shown that individuals who engage in internally directed impulsive behaviors are more likely to experience and express anger relatively frequently and without specific provocation (Milligan and Waller, 2001).

POOR CONSIDERATION OF CONSEQUENCES IN THE FUTURE

Consideration of future consequences (CFC) is thinking about future outcomes of one's current behavior (Strathman et al., 1994). People who do not consider the outcomes of their current behavior are more likely to engage in aggressive behavior.

- When people are angry, they are less likely to consider the future outcomes of their behavior (Joiremen et al., 2003).
- Aggressive children and adolescents generate more aggression and have fewer constructive potential solutions to an interpersonal conflict and they do not anticipate the long-term consequences of their aggressive acts.
- High level of consideration of consequences in the future is associated with low levels of anger (Joireman et al., 2003), less driving anger, and less risky driving (Moore and Dahlen, 2008). Moore and Dahlen found that individuals with high CFC expressed driving-related anger in an appropriate manner. Therefore, CFC can be an effective strategy in effectively coping with everyday anger experienced by a layman.

SUMMARY

Thus we see that anger has a widespread impact in every sphere of life. Traffic accidents, marital conflicts, dating violence, sports aggression, and workplace aggression are the major problems in today's fast growing industrialized society. As we have seen, anger is the root cause of all such problems, therefore, anger management at every stage of life is very much important for a healthy and wealthy life. To unfold the root cause of above-mentioned problems, anger management techniques for self, family, school, and workplace have been described in the next section of the book.

REFERENCES

Adolphs, R., Tranel, D., Hamann, S., Young, A. W., Calder, A. J., Phelps, E. A., Anderson, A., Lee, G. P., and Damasio, A. R. (1999). 'Recognition of Facial Emotion in Nine Individuals with Bilateral Amygdala Damage', *Neuropsychologia*, 37: 1111–17.

Anderson, E. (1978). *A Place on the Corner*, Chicago: University of Chicago Press.

Andersson, L. M., and Pearson, C. M. (1999). 'Tit for Tat? The Spiraling Effect of Incivility in the Workplace', *Academy of Management Review*, 24: 452–71.

Arnett, J. J., Offer, D., and Fine, M. A. (1997). 'Reckless Driving in Adolescence: "State" and Trait: Factors', *Accident Analysis and Prevention*, 29: 57–63.

Averill, J. R. (1982). *Anger and Aggression: An Essay on Emotions*. New York: Springer-Verlag.

Bagner, D. M., Stroch, E. A., and Preston, A. S. (2007). 'Romantic Relational Aggression: What about Gender?', *Journal of Family Violence*, 22: 19–24.

Baker, F., Johnson, M. W., and Bickel, W. K. (2003). 'Delay Discounting in Current and Never-before Cigarette Smokers: Similarities and Differences across Commodity, Sign, and Magnitude', *Journal of Abnormal Psychology*, 112(3): 382–92.

Baker, J. D., Williamson, D. A., and Sylve, C. (1995). 'Body Image Disturbance, Memory Bias, and Body Dysphoria: Effects of Negative Mood Induction', *Behavior Therapy*, 26: 747–59.

Baldaro, B., Gattacchi, M. W., Codispoti, M., and Tuozzi, G. (1996) 'Modification of Electrogastrographic Activity During the Viewing of Brief Film Sequences', *Perceptual and Motor Skills*, 82(ii): 1243–50.

Barsade, S. G. (2002). 'The Ripple Effect: Emotional Contagion and its Influence on Group Behavior', *Administrative Science Quarterly*, 47: 644–75.

Berkowitz, L. (2001). 'Affect, Aggression, and Antisocial Behavior', in R. J. Davidson, K. Scherer, and H. H. Goldsmith (eds.), *Handbook of Affective Sciences*, (pp. 804–23). New York/Oxford UK: Oxford University Press.

Bhavisha D., Pekkala, D., Allen, D., and Cummins, P. (2006). 'Gender and Anger', in Peter, C. (ed.), *Working with Anger*, (pp. 149–58). England: John Wiley and Sons, Ltd.

Bhagat, R., and Allie, S. (1989). 'Organizational Stress, Personal Life Stress and Symptoms of Life Strain: An Examination of the Moderating Role of a Sense of Competence', *Journal of Vocational Behaviour*, 35: 231–53.

Bianchi, E. C. (1976). 'The Super-bowl Culture of Male Violence', in D. F. Sabo and R. Runfola (eds), *Jock Sports and Male Identity*. Englewood Cliffs, NJ: Prentice-Hall.

Bies, R. J., Tripp, T. M., and Kramer, R. M. (1997). 'At the Breaking Point: Cognitive and Social Dynamics of Revenge in Organizations', in R. A. Giacalone and J. Greenberg, (eds), *Antisocial Behavior in Organizations* (pp. 18–36). Thousand Oaks, CA: Sage.

Bihldorff, J. P., King, S. H., and Parnes, L. R. (1971). 'Psychological Factors in Headache', *Headache*, 11: 117–27.

Boccialetti, G. (1988). Teambuilding: Blueprints for Productivity and Satisfaction. *Teams and the Management of Emotion*. NTL Institute Alexandria, VA and Pfeiffer, San Diego, 62–67.

Boergers, J., Spirito, A., and Donaldson, D. (1998). Reasons for Adolescent Suicide Attempts: Associations with Psychological Functioning. *Journal of the American Academy of Child and Adolescent Psychiatry*, 37: 1287–93.

Breuer, J., and Freud, S. (1956). *Studies on Hysteria*. J. Strachey and A. Strachey, trans., London: Hogarth Press.

Briere, J., and Malamuth, N. (1983). 'Self-reported Likelihood of Sexually Aggressive Behavior: Attitedinal vs Sexual Explanations', *Journal of Research in Personality*, 17: 315–23.

Brosschot, J. F, and Thayer, J. F. (2004). 'Worry, Perseverative Thinking and Health', in Nyklícek I, Temoshok L, Vingerhoets A, (eds.), *Emotional Expression and Health. Advances in Theory, Assessment and Clinical Applications*. Hove: Brunner-Routledge.

Burns, J. W., Johnson, B. J., Devine, J., Mahoney, N., and Pawl, R. (1998). 'Anger Management Style and the Prediction of Treatment Outcome among Male and Female Chronic Pain Patients', *Behav. Res. Ther.*, 36: 1051–62.

Buss, D. M. (1987). 'Selection, Evocation, and Manipulation', *Journal of Personality and Social Psychology*, 53: 1214–21.

Calhoun, P. S., Bosworth, H. B., Siegler, I. C., and Bastian, L. A. (2001). 'The Relationship between Hostility and Behavioral Risk Factors for Poor Health in Women Veterans', *Preventive.Medicine*, 33: 552–57.

Chang, P. P., Ford, D. E., Meoni, L. A., Wang, N. Y., and Klag, M. J. (2002). 'Anger in Young Men and Subsequent Premature Cardiovascular Disease: The Precursors Study', *Arch. Intern. Med.*, 162: 901–06.

Chen, P. Y., and Spector, P. E. (1992). 'Relationships of Work Stressors with Aggression, Withdrawal, Theft and Substance Use: An Exploratory Study', *Journal of Occupational Psychology*, 65: 177–84.

Crick, N. R., and Grotpeter, J. K. (1995). 'Relational Aggression, Gender, and Social-Psychological Adjustment', *Child Development*, 66: 710–22.

Davidson, R. J., Abercrombie, H., Nitschke, J. B., Putnam, K. (1999). 'Regional Brain Function, Emotion and Disorders of Emotion', *Curr. Opin. Neurobiol.*, 9: 228–34.

Davidson, R. J., Putnam, K. M., and Larson, C. L. (2000). 'Dysfunction in the Neural Circuitry of Emotion Regulation—A Possible Prelude to Violence', *Science 2000*, 289: 591–94.

Deffenbacher, J. L., Oetting, E. R., Lynch, R. S., and Morris, C. D. (1996). 'The Expression of Anger and its Consequences', *Behavior Research Therapy*, 34(7): 575–90.

Deffenbacher, J. L., Deffenbacher, D. M., Lynch, R. S., and Richards, T. L. (2003). 'Anger, Aggression, and Risky Behavior: A Comparison of High and Low Anger Drivers', *Behav. Res. Ther.*, 41: 701–18.

Dodge, K. A. (1991). 'The Structure and Function of Reactive and Proactive Aggression', in D. J. Pepler and K. H. Rubin (eds.), *The Development and Treatment of Childhood Aggression* (pp. 201–18). Hillsdale: Erlbaum.

Drossman, D. A. (1999). 'The Functional Gastrointestinal Disorders and the Rome II Process', *Gut*, 45 (SII) 1–5.

Dutton, D. G. (1999). 'Traumatic Origins of Intimate Rage', *Aggression Violent Behavior*, 4: 431–47.

Edman, J. L., Yates, A., Aruguete, M. S., and DeBord, K. A. (2005). 'Negative Emotion and Disordered Eating among Obese College Students', *Eating Behavior*, 6(4): 308–17.

Ellsworth, P. C., and Tong, E. M. W. (2007). 'What does it Mean to be Angry at Yourself? Categories, Appraisals, and the Problem of Language' *Emotion*, 6: 572–86.

Engel, G. L. (1959). '"Psychogenic" Pain and the Pain-prone Patient', *American Journal of Medicine*, 20: 899–918.

Everson, S. A., Kaplan, G. A., Goldberg, D. E., Lakka, T. A., Sivenius, J., and Salonen, J. T. (1999). 'Anger Expression and Incident Stroke: Prospective Evidence from the Kuopio Ischemic Heart Disease Study', *Stroke*, 30: 523–28.

Diamond, E. (1982). 'The Role of Anger and Hostility in Essential Hypertension and Coronary Heart Disease', *Psychological Bulletin*, 92: 410–33.

Duckro, P. N., Chibnall, J. T., and Tomazic, T. J. (1995). 'Anger, Depression, and Disability: A Path Analysis of Relationships in a Sample of Chronic Posttraumatic Headache Patients', *Headache*, 35: 7–9.

Friedman, H., and Booth-Kewley, S. (1987). 'The "Disease-prone Personality": A Meta-analytic View of the Construct', *American Psychologist*, 42: 539–55.

Frijda, N. H. (1986). *The Emotions*. New York, NY: Cambridge University Press.

Futterman, L. G., and Lemberg, L. (2002). 'Anger and Acute Coronary Events', *American Journal of Critical Care*, 11: 574–76.

Garssen, B., and Goodkin, K. (2001). 'Psychological Factors and Cancer Progression: Involvement of Neuroimmune Pathways and Future Directions for Laboratory Research', in C. E. Lewis, R. M. O. O'Brien, and J. Barraclough (eds.), *The Psychoimmunology of Cancer* (pp. 209–34). Oxford: Oxford University Press.

Gaskin, M. E., Greene, A. F., Robinson, M. E., and Geisser, M. E. (1992). 'Negative Affect and the Experience of Chronic Pain', *Journal of Psychosomatic Research*, 36: 707–13.

Glomb, T. M. (2002). 'Workplace Anger and Aggression: Informing Conceptual Models with Data from Specific Encounters', *Journal of Occupational Health Psychology*, 7: 20–36.

Golden, S. H., Williams, J. E., Ford, D. E., Yeh, H. C., Stanford, C. P., Nieto, F. J., and Brancati. F. L. (2006). 'Anger Temperament is Modestly Associated with the Risk of Type 2 Diabetes Mellitus: The Atheroslcerosis Risk in Communities Study', *Psychoneuroendocrinology*, 31(3): 325–32.

Gould, R. A., Ball, S., and Kaspi, S. P. (1996). 'Prevalence and Correlates of Anger Attacks: A Two Site Study', *Journal of Affective Disorder*, 39: 31–38.

Grunbaum, J. A., Vernon, S. W., and Clasen, C. M. (1997). 'The Association between Anger and Hostility and Risk Factors for Coronary Heart Disease in Children and Adolescents: A Review', *Ann. Behav. Med.*, 19: 179–89.

Harburg, E., Julius, M., Kaciroti, N., Gleiberman, L., and Schork, M. (2003). 'Expressive/Suppressive Anger-coping Responses, Gender, and Type of Mortality: A 17-year Follow-up (Tecumseh, Michigan, 1971–1988)', *Psychosomatic Medicine*, 65: 588–97.

Hatch, J. P., Schoenfeld, L. S., Boutros, N. N., Seleshi, E., Moore, P. J., and Cur-Provost, M. (2005). 'Anger and Hostility in Tension-type Headache', *Headache*, 31(5): 302–04.

Hazebroek, J., Howells, K., and Day, A. (2001). 'Cognitive Appraisals Associated with High Trait Anger. *Personality and Individual Differences'*, 30: 31–45.

Hokanson, J. E., and Butler, A. C. (1992). 'Cluster Analysis of Depressed College Students' Social Behaviors', *Journal of Personality and Social Psychology*, 62: 273–80.

Horn, R., and Towl, G. (1997). 'Anger Management for Women Prisoners. *Issues in Criminological and Legal Psychology'*, 29: 57–62.

Jamner, L. D., Shapiro, D., and Goldstein, I. H. U. G. (1991). 'Ambulatory Blood Pressure and Heart Rate in Paramedics: Effects of Cynical Hostility and Defensiveness', *Psychosomatic Medicine*, 53: 393–406.

Johnson, E. H. (unpublished). *Anger and Anxiety as Determinants of Elevated Blood Pressure in Adolescents: The Tampa Study*. doctoral dissertation. University of South Florida, Tampa.

———. (1990). *The Deadly Emotions: The Role of Anger, Hostility, and Aggression in Health and Emotional Well-being*. New York: Praeger Publishers.

Johnson-Saylor, M. T. (1991). 'Psychosocial Predictors of Healthy Behaviours in Women', *Journal of Advanced Nursing*, 16: 1164–71.

Joireman, J., Anderson, J., Strathman, A. (2003). 'The Aggression Paradox: Understanding Links among Aggression, Sensation Seeking, and the Consideration of Future Consequences'. *Journal of Personality and Social Psychology*, 84(6): 1287–1302.

Karasawa, K. (2003). 'Interpersonal Reactions toward Depression and Anger', *Cognition and Emotion*, 17, 123–38.

Kashani, J. H., Suarez, L., Allan, W., and Reid, J. C. (1997). 'Hopelessness in Inpatient Youths: A Closer Look at Behavior, Emotional Expression, and Social Support', *Journal of the American Academy of Child and Adolescent Psychiatry*, 36: 1625–31.

Kassinove, H., and Sukhodolsky, D. G. (1995). 'Anger Disorder: Basic Science and Practice Issues', in H. Kassinove (ed.), *Anger Disorders: Definition, Diagnosis, and Treatment* (pp. 1–26). Washington, DC: Taylor & Francis.

Kassinove, H., and Tafrate, R. C. (2002). *Anger Management: The Complete Treatment Guidebook for Practitioners.* California: Impact Publishers.

Keinan, G. (1987). 'Decision Making under Stress: Scanning of Alternatives under Controllable and Uncontrollable Threats', *Journal of Personality and Social Psychology*, 52: 639–44.

Kerns, R. D., Rosenberg, R., and Jacob, M. C. (2005). 'Anger Expression and Chronic Pain', *Journal of Behavioral Medicine*, 17: 57–67.

Knox, S. S., Siegmund, K. D., Weidner, G., Ellison, R. C., Adelman, A., and Paton, C. (1998). 'Hostility, Social Support, and Coronary Heart Disease in the National Heart, Lung, and Blood Institute Family Heart Study', *American Journal of Cardiology*, 82: 1192–96.

Koh, K., Choe, K., and An, S. (2003). 'Anger and Coronary Calcification in Individuals with and Without Risk Factors or Coronary Artery Disease', *Yonsei Medical Journal*, 44: 793–99.

Kubzansky, L. D., Sparrow, D., Jackson, B., Cohen, S., Weiss, S. T., Wright, R. J. (2006). 'Angry Breathing: A Prospective Study of Hostility and Lung Function in the Normative Aging Study', *Thorax*, 61: 863–68.

Lawton, R., and Nutter, A. (2002). 'A Comparison of Reported Levels and Expression of Anger in Everyday and Driving Situations', *British Journal of Psychology*, 93: 407–23.

Lieberman, M. A., and Goldstein, B. A. (2005). 'Not all Negative Emotions are Equal: The Role of Emotional Expression in Online Support Groups for Women with Breast Cancer', *Psychooncology*, 15: 160–68.

Lohr, J. M., and Hamberger, K. L. (1990). 'Cognitive-behavioral Modification of Coronary-prone Behaviors: Proposal for a Treatment Model and Review of the Evidence', *Journal of Rational-Emotive and Cognitive-Behavior Therapy*, 8: 103–26.

Lombardo, E. R., Tan, G., Jensen, M. P., and Anderson, K. O. (2005). 'Anger Management Style and Associations with Self-efficacy and Pain in Male Veterans', *The Journal of Pain*, 6: 765–70.

Mammen, O. K., Shear, M. K., Pilkonis, P. A., Kolko, D. J., Thase, M. E., and Greeno, C. G. (1999). 'Anger Attacks: Correlates and Significance of an Underrecognized Symptom', *Journal of Clinical Psychiatry*, 60: 633–42.

Mason, C. A., Walker-Barnes, C. J., Tu, S., Simons, J., and Martinez-Arrue, R. (2004). 'Ethnic Differences in the Affective Meaning of Parental Control Behaviors', *Journal of Primary Prevention*, 25: 59–79.

Materazzo, F., Cathart, S., and Pritchard, D. (2000). 'Anger, Depression, and Coping Interactions in Headache Activity and Adjustment: A Controlled Study', *J. Psychosom. Res.*, 49: 69–75.

Merskey, H., and Spear, F. G. (1967). *Pain: Psychological and Psychiatric Aspects.* London: Bailliere, Tindall, Cassell.

Mikulincer, M. (1998). 'Adult Attachment Style and Individual Differences in Functional versus Dysfunctional Experiences of Anger', *Journal of Personality and Social Psychology*, 74: 513–24.

Miller, T. Q., Marksides, K. S., Chiriboga, D. A., and Ray, L. A. (1995). 'A Test of the Psychosocial Vulnerability and Health Behavior Models of Hostility: Results from an 11-year Follow-up Study of Mexican Americans', *Psychosomatic Medicine*, 57: 572–81.

Milligan, R. J., and Waller, G. (2001). 'Anger and Impulsivity in Non-clinical Women', *Journal of Personality and Individual Differences*, 30: 1073–78.

Moore, M., and Dahlen, E. R. (2008). 'Forgiveness and Consideration of Future Consequences in Aggressive Driving', *Accident Analysis and Prevention*, 40: 1661–66.

Morris, T., Greer, S., Pettingale, K. W., and Watson, M. (1981). 'Patterns of Expression of Anger and their Psychological Correlates in Women with Breast Cancer', *Journal of Psychosomatic Research,* 25: 111–17.

Morris, C. D., Deffenbacher, J. L., Lynch, R. S., and Oetting, E. R. (1996, August). '*Anger Expression and its Consequences*, paper presented at the 104th Annual Convention of the American Psychological Association, Toronto, Ontario, Canada.

Moscovitch, D. A., McCabe, R. E., Antony, M. M., Rocca, L., and Swinson, R. P. (2007). 'Anger Experience and Expression across the Anxiety Disorder' *Depression and Anxiety.*

Mueller, W. H., Grunbaum, J. A., and Labarthe, R. R. (2001). 'Anger Expression, Body Fat, and Blood Pressure in Adolescents: Project Heartbeat!', *American Journal of Human Biology,* 13(4): 531–38.

Newton, T. L., and Kiecolt-Glaser, J. K. (1995). 'Hostility and Erosion of Marital Quality During Early Marriage', *Journal of Behavioral Medicine,* 18: 601–19.

Nicholson, R. A., Gramling, S. E., Ong, J. C., and Buenevar, L. (2003). 'Differences in Anger Expression between Individuals With and Without Headache after Controlling for Depression and Anxiety', *Headache,* 43: 651–63.

Novaco, R. (1991). 'Aggression on Roadways', in R., Baenninger (ed.), *Targets of Violence and Aggression.* North Holland: Elsevier.

Novaco, R. W. (2003). *The Novaco Anger Scale and Provocation Inventory (NAS-PI).* Los Angeles, CA: Western Psychological Services.

Novaco, R. W., and Jarvis, K. L. (2002). 'Brief Cognitive Behavioral Intervention for Anger', in F. Bond and W. Dryden (eds), *Handbook of Brief Cognitive Behavioral Therapy.* pp. 77–100. London: John Wiley.

Parkinson, B. (1999). 'Relations and Dissociations between Appraisal and Emotion Ratings of Reasonable and Unreasonable Anger and Guilt', *Cognition and Emotion,* 13: 347–85.

Patton, J. H., Stanford, M. S., and Barratt, E. S. (1995). 'Factor Structure of the Barratt Impulsiveness Scale', *Journal of Clinical Psychology,* 51(6): 768–74.

Patricia, M., Fitzmaurice, G., Kubzansky, L. D., Eric, B., Rimm, E. B., and Kawachi, I. (2003). 'Anger Expression and Risk of Stroke and Coronary Heart Disease among Male Health Professionals', *Psychosomatic Medicine,* 65: 100–10.

Pauls, C. A., and Stemmler, G. (2003). 'Repressive and Defensive Coping during Fear and Anger', *Emotion,* 3: 284–302.

Peveler, R. C., and Johnston, D. W. (2002). 'Subjective and Cognitive Effects of Relaxation', *Behavioral Research Therapy,* 24: 413–19.

Pilowsky, I. (1986). 'Psychodynamic Aspects of the Pain Experience', in R. A. Stembach (ed.), *The Psychology of Pain* (2nd ed., pp. 181–96). New York: Raven Press.

Prigerson, H. G., and Slimack, M. J. (1999). 'Gender Differences in Clinical Correlates of Suicidality among Young Adults', *Journal of Nervous and Mental Disease,* 187: 23–31.

Raine, A. (1993). *The Psychopathology of Crime: Criminal Behavior as a Clinical Disorder.* Academic Press, San Diego.

Robins, S., and Novaco, R. W. (2000). 'Anger Control as a Health Promotion Mechanism', in D. I. Mostofsky and D. H. Barlow (eds.), *The Management of Anxiety in Medical Disorders.* Boston: Allyn and Bacon, pp. 361–77.

Rosenberg, E., Ekman, P., Jiang, W., Babyak, M., Coleman, R., Hanson, M., O'Connor C., Waugh R., and Blumenthal, J. A. (2001). 'Linkages between Facial Expressions of Anger and Transient Myocardial Ischemia in Men with Coronary Artery Disease', *Emotion,* 1, 107–15.

Saini, S. (2006). 'Body Dissatisfaction and Psychological Problems', *Asian Journal of Pediatric Practice,* 10(1): 47–53.

Saini, S. (2007). 'Suicidal Ideation among Adolescents', *Asian Journal of Pediatric Practices.*

———. (2008a). 'Romantic Relational Aggression and Psychosocial Problems among Adolescents', *International Society for the Study of Behavioral Disorders Newsletter*, 53(1): 5–8.

———. (2008b). 'Driving Aggression among Adolescents', *Asian Journal of Pediatric Practices*, 11(3): 5–10.

———. (2009). 'Anger, Hostility and Aggression: The AHA-Syndrome', *The AHA-Syndrome and Cardiovascular Diseases* (pp. 1–15) in Swati, B. and Sunil, S. (eds.). New Delhi: Anamaya Publication Ltd.

———. (2009a). 'Agression in Relation to Sensation Seeking and Impulsivity'. Unpublished Doctoral thesis, Department of Psychology, Punjab University, Patiala.

Saini, S., and Bhave, S. (2008). 'Sports Aggression', *Handbook of Sports Medicine in Children and Adolescents* in Swati, B. (ed.). New Delhi: Jaypee Brothers Medical Publishers.

Saini, S., Jaswant, S., and Kiran, A. (2008). *Psychological Aggression among Marital Relationships.* Paper Presented at National Conference Organized by Department of Applied Psychology, GJUST, Hisar, Haryana.

Saini, S., and Trama, S. forthcoming. *Aggression in Relation to Sensation Seeking, Impulsivity and CFC: A Cross-cultural Comparison.*

Scheier, L. M., and Botvin, G. J. (1997). 'Psychosocial Correlates of Affective Distress: Latent-variable Models of Male and Female Adolescents in a Community Sample', *Journal of Youth Adolescent*, 26: 89–115.

Scherwitz, L., and Rugulies, R. (1992). 'Life-style and Hostility', in H. S. Friedman (ed.), *Hostility, Coping and Health* (pp. 77–98). Washington, DC: American Psychological Association.

Schnall, P. L., Schwartz, J. E., Landsbergis, P. A., Warren, K., and Pickering, T. O. (1998). 'A Longitudinal Study of Job Strain and Ambulatory Blood Pressure: Results from a Three-year Follow-up', *Psychosomatic Medicine*, 60: 697–706.

Siegman, A. W. (1994). *Anger, Hostility, and the Heart* (pp. 1–22, 173–198). Hillsdale, NJ: Lawrence Erlbaum Associates.

Siegman, A. W., Malkin, A. R., Boyle, S., Vaitkus, M., Barko, W., and Franco, E. (2002). 'Anger, and Plasma Lipid, Lipoprotein, and Glucose Levels in Healthy Women: The Mediating Role of Physical Fitness', *Journal of Behavioral. Medicine*, 25: 1–16.

Sigelrnan, C. K., Berry, C. J., and Wiles, K. A. (1984). 'Violence in College Students' Dating Relationships', *Journal of Applied Social Psychology*, 14: 530–48.

Smith, T. W., and Allred, K. D. (1989). 'Blood-pressure Responses during Social Interaction in High- and Low-cynically Hostile Males', *Journal of Behavioral Medicine*, 12: 135–43.

Spector, P. E. (1997). 'The Role of Frustration in Antisocial Behavior at Work', in R. A. Giacalone, J. and Greenberg (eds.), *Antisocial Behavior in Organizations* (pp.1–17). Sage: Thousand Oaks, CA.

Spielberger, C. D., Jacobs, G., Russell, S., and Crane, R. (1983). 'Assessment of Anger: The State-Trait Anger Scale (STAS)', in J. N. Butcher and C. D. Spielberger (eds.), *Advances in Personality Assessment* Vol. 2, (pp. 159–87). Lawrence Erlbaum Associates, Inc., Hillsdale, New Jersey.

Spielberger, C. D. (1996). *State-Trait Anger Expression Inventory.* Research Edition: Professional Manual. Florida: Psychological Assessment Resources.

———. (1999). *State-Trait Anger Expression Inventory-2* (Professional Manual). Lutz, FL: Psychological Assessment Resources.

Spielberger, C. D., Reheiser, E. C., and Sydeman, S. J. (1995). 'Measuring the Experience, Expression and Control of Anger', in H. Kassinove (ed.), *Anger Disorders: Definitions, Diagnosis, and Treatment* (pp. 49–67). Washington, D.C: Taylor & Francis.

Spielberger, C. D., Ritterband, L. M., Sydeman, S. J., Reheiser, E. C., and Unger, K. K. (1995). 'Assessment of Emotional States and Personality Traits: Measuring Psychological Vital Things', in N. J. Butcher (ed.), *Clinical Personality Assessment: Practical Approaches* (pp. 42–58). New York, NY: Oxford University Press.

Stein, D., Apter, A., Ratzoni, G., Har-Even, D., and Avidan, G. (1998). 'Association between Multiple Suicide Attempts and Negative Affects in Adolescents', *Journal of the American Academy of Child and Adolescent Psychiatry*, 37: 488–94.

Steptoe, A. (1984). 'Psychological Aspects of Bronchial Asthma', in Rachman S. (ed.), *Contributions to Medical Psychology* Vol. 3, (7–30). Elmsford, NY: Pergamon Press.

Stice, E. (2001). 'A Prospective Test of the Dual Pathway Model of Bulimic Pathology: Mediating Effects of Dieting and Negative Affect', *J. Abnor. Psychol.*, 110: 124–35.

Strathman, A., Gleicher, F., Boninger, D., and Edwards, C. S. (1994). 'The Consideration of Future Consequences: Weighing Immediate and Distant Outcomes of Behavior', *Journal of Personality and Social Psychology*, 66: 742–52.

Suchday, S., and Larkin, K. T. (2001). 'Biobehavioral Responses to Interpersonal Conflict during Anger Expression among Anger-in and Anger-out Men', *Ann. Behav. Med.*, 23: 282–90.

Suls, J., Wan, C. K., and Costa, P. T. (1995). 'Relationship of Trait Anger to Resting Blood Pressure: A Meta-analysis', *Health Psychology*, 14: 444–56.

Suarez, E. C. (2006). 'Sex Differences in the Relation of Depressive Symptoms, Hostility, and Anger Expression to Indices of Glucose Metabolism in Nondiabetic Adults', *Health Psychology*, 4: 484–92.

Summers, J. D., Rapoff, M. A., Varghese, G., Porter, K., and Palmer, R. E. (1991). 'Psychosocial Factors in Chronic Spinal Cord Injury Pain', *Pain*, 47: 183–89.

Tafrate, R. C., Kassinove, H., and Dundin, L. (2002). 'Anger Episodes in High- and Low-trait-Anger Community Adults', *Journal of Clinical Psychology*, 58: 1573–90.

Taft, C. T., O'Farrell, T. J., Torres, S. E., Panuzio, J., Monson, C. M., Murphy, M., and Murphy, C. M. (2006). 'Examining the Correlates of Psychological Aggression among a Community Sample of Couples', *Journal of Family Psychology*, 20(4): 581–84.

Tarter, R. E., Blackson, T., Brigham, J., Moss, H., and Caprara, G. V. (1995). 'The Association between Childhood Irritability and Liability to Substance Use in Early Adolescence: A 2-year Follow-up Study of Boys at Risk for Substance Abuse', *Drug Alcohol Dependence*, 39: 253–61.

Tavris, C. (1989). *Anger: The Misunderstood Emotion* (rev. ed). New York: Touchstone.

Taylor, M. J., and Cooper, P. J. (1992). 'An Experimental Study of the Effects of Mood on Body Size Perception', *Behavior Research and Therapy*, 30: 53–58.

Temoshok, L., and Dreher, H. (1992). '*The Type C Connection: The Mind–Body Links to Cancer and Your Health'*, New York: Plume.

Thomas, S., Groer, M., Davis, M., Droppleman, P., Mozingo, J., and Pierce, M. (2000). 'Anger and Cancer: An Analysis of the Linkages', *Cancer Nursing*, 23: 344–49.

Ulrich, R. S., Simons, R. F., Losito, B. D., Fiorito, E., Miles, M. A., and Zelson, M. (1991). 'Stress Recovery During Exposure to Natural and Urban Environments', *Journal of Environmental Psychology*, 11: 201–30.

van Eck, M., Berkhof, H., Nicolson, N., and Sulon, J. (1996). 'The Effects of Perceived Stress, Traits, Mood States, and Stressful Daily Events on Salivary Cortisol', *Psychosomatic Medicine*, 58: 447–58.

Venable, V. L., Carlson, C. R., and Wilson, J. (2001). The Role of Anger and Depression in Recurrent Headache', *Headache*, 41: 21–30.

Wade, J. B., Price, D. D., Hamer, R. M., Schwartz, S. M., and Hart, R. P. (1990). An Emotional Component Analysis of Chronic Pain', *Pain*, 40: 303–10.

Waller, G., Babbs, M., Milligan, R., Meyer, C., Ohanian, V., and Leung, N. (2003). 'Anger and Core Beliefs in the Eating Disorders', *International Journal of Eating Disorders*, 34: 118–24.

Watson J. M., Cascardi, M., Avery-Leaf, S., and O'Leary, K. D. (2001). 'High School Students Responses to Dating Aggression', *Violence and Victims,* 16(3): 339–48.

Welgan, P., and Meshkinpour, H. (2000). 'Role of Anger in Antral Motor Activity in Irritable Bowl Syndrome (IBS)', *Digestive Diseases and Sciences*, 45: 248–51.

Wertheim, E. H., Koerner, J., and Paxton, S. (2001). 'Longitudinal Predictors of Restrictive Eating and Bulimic Tendencies in Three Different Age Groups of Adolescent Girls', *J. Youth Adolescence*, 30: 69–81.

Whitehead, W. E., Engle, B. T., and Shuster, M. (1980). 'Irritable Bowel Syndrome, Physiological and Psychological Differences between Diarrhea-predominant and Constipation-predominant Patients', *Digestive Diseases and Sciences*, 25: 404–13.

Wolfe, D. A., and Feiring, C. (2000). 'Dating Violence through the Lens of Adolescent Romantic Relationships', *Child Maltreatment*, 5: 360–63.

Wright, R., Rodriquez, M., and Cohen, S. (1998). 'Review of Psychosocial Stress and Asthma: An Integrated Biopsychosocial Approach', *Thorax*, 53: 1066–74.

Zuckerman, M. (1979). *Sensation Seeking: Beyond the Optimal Level of Arousal.* Hillsdale, NJ: Lawrence Erlbaum.

SECTION THREE

Dealing with Anger

ANGER MANAGEMENT

In the day-to-day life there are countless examples of experiencing anger in oneself or bearing the brunt of anger expressed by others.

Box 3.1 Aristotle's Five Rights in Anger

- With the right person
- To the right degree
- At the right time
- For the right purpose
- In the right way

With the right person: To maintain discipline as a job responsibility certain situations make a person get angry with another person: parents with children, teachers with students, bosses with employees, etc.

To the right degree: However it should not be excessive and there should not be an overreaction to trivial matters.

At the right time: The anger should not be misplaced and should be expressed at the time when it will yield results and not humiliate or insult the other person nor put him on the defensive, leading him to rebel.

For the right purpose: Anger against injustice is a very purposeful anger. It should be shown for constructive purposes to improve things or persons. If the opposite is achieved then anger is not justified.

In the right way: Anger is meant to show that something is wrong and should be corrected. Being violent, destructive, abusive, threatening, humiliating, etc. is not the right way to express anger. Displeasure conveyed in a calm assertive way gets better results.

Anger is not justified if

- it is selfishly motivated;
- lingers on for a long time;
- attacks a person instead of the issue.

WHY DOES ONE GET ANGRY THOUGHTS?

Events do not make a person angry but the interpretation of these provokes anger.

- People who do not have an open mind and have a lot of prejudice and suspicion against others end up getting angry very frequently and unjustifiably.
- Persons who have an angry temperament, anger is constantly lurking in the mind and the slightest provocation land them into volatile anger.

HOW TO CONTROL ANGRY THOUGHTS?

- Admit you are angry–very difficult for people who have a lot of ego.
- Analyze and identify the source of your anger–often the real problem is very minor but is confused with other negative feelings or emotions you are already harboring against the person concerned.
- Analyze your anger emotion: why are you feeling angry?
- Analyze the reason for your feelings of anger.
- Analyze if your anger is justifiable or reasonable? If unreasonable you can diffuse your feelings.

WHY DO WE NEED TO MANAGE OUR ANGER?

We have discussed this in detail in the first two sections but let us recapitulate some important aspects. Feeling angry is a normal reaction, which is functional for an individual but when it leads to behaviors like aggression and violence, it becomes a source of distress to the individual and others.

People do not generally understand the long-term emotional distress and physical ill effects caused by anger and they continue to bear the negative consequences of anger.

Anger is a major cause of straining and often spoiling inter-personal relations. In a fit of rage, a man can spoil or destroy a good relationship, which have taken 'ages' to be built, in a matter of few seconds or minutes. By losing one's patience and self-control, a provocative situation is created for self and for others.

Anger hampers growth, productivity, and effectiveness. It hampers work output whether in the family or workplace. It incapacitates a person from seeing things from the right perspective, rationally, and objectively.

Hence anger management or learning to control your anger is a must for every human being, be it a small child, a young person, or an elderly citizen. It is important to handle your anger in a positive manner. If you learn some basic anger management techniques then you can get a sense of self-control over your inner or external responses to various situations.

FIRST STEP TOWARD ANGER MANAGEMENT IS AN HONEST SELF-ANALYSIS

Analyze what is making you angry.

We get angry because certain personal needs are not met. What we are really feeling is anxiety, sadness, and fear over our unmet needs. But those feelings come out as anger because we feel helpless and don't know any other way to get our needs met. In actuality, losing temper works against us because in such a situation it is less likely that our needs will be met.

THE CAPACITY OR ABILITY TO GET ANGRY VARIES GREATLY

Some people feel angry most of the time, whereas others report feeling angry very rarely. A person with continuous episodes of anger has a five-time greater chance of dying before the age of 50. Anger elevates blood pressure, increases risk of stroke, heart disease, cancer, depression, and other physiological problems (Everson et al., 1999; Futterman and Lemberg, 2002; Thomas et al., 2000). Do you find yourself becoming angry at very trivial things? How do you react when your child changes the TV channel you are watching or interrupts your reading? Do you show irritation when your wife tells you to do some domestic chore when you are planning a leisure activity?

Make a List of Things that Make You Angry

- Make separate lists for home, work, and your social outings.
- Then you can identify if there are some unmet needs and the feelings you have regarding these.

Once the true feelings have been analyzed then they can be constructively expressed, instead of losing one's temper.

Figure 3.1 Analyze your anger and the angry situations you have been in

- Make a list by recall: how many times you got angry each day in the last one week.
- Then keep a diary to note down daily how many times you are getting angry in the coming week.

Make a Detailed Analysis of Each Episode of Anger—Both Past and Present

- What made you angry?
- Who made you angry?
- Where did you get angry?
- How long did your anger last?
- How did you behave?
- How did you feel?
- Whom did you hurt emotionally?
- Whom did you get into a fight with?
- In retrospect, could you have controlled your anger?
- Could you have dealt with the situation differently?
- Do you feel your anger was justified?
- Did it achieve a purpose such as establishing discipline in home or office?
- Was it a misplaced anger i.e., you were angry about something else but took your anger out on the wrong person or at the wrong time?
- What has your anger resulted in?

- Have you caused harm to your office relationship or your career?
- Have you caused hurt to your spouse or family?
- How did you feel after the episode was over? Happy and victorious? Or, ashamed and guilty?
- Do you wish this event had not happened?
- Would you like to apologize to the persons concerned?
- Do you have any regrets?
- You want to apologize but your ego is coming in the way?

We need to accept that anger management requires training and we need not be ashamed to take professional help.

Figure 3.2 If you do not shout or show your anger then are you in control of your anger?

Some people do not express their anger and feel they are having control over their anger but do not realize that they are harming themselves. If you hold in your anger, you may not hurt others, unless they sense your withdrawal or unspoken irritation, but it will certainly hurt you. Studies show that people who let anger build up inside them tend to suffer more health problems than those who have less anger or manage it in productive ways (Kassinove and Tafrate, 2002).

So it is important not to feel angry all the time as it harms your mind and body, whether you express it outwardly or bottle it up inside you.

The technique of 'Anger management' is needed to help people to learn how to reduce the emotional and physiological arousals caused by anger.

AIMS OF ANGER MANAGEMENT

- By learning to manage one's anger, one can deal with, and expel the negative responses and emotions, before it causes any discomfort to self and others.
- Anger management techniques have been very effective in controlling anger and aggression among children, adolescents, and adults.

- Many anger management techniques are easy to learn and practice, so give them a try before losing your temper unnecessarily again.

This chapter emphasizes on anger management tips for self-improvement.

THE BAD EFFECTS OF ANGER

Anger affects human beings in a variety of ways. Some of these ill effects are the following:

- Decreased work output.
- Disturbed mental and psychological balance can cause depression.
- Inability to focus on work, as anger causes disturbance and distraction.
- Inability to think rationally.
- Inadequate human relation skills.
- Increased risk of physical illness like cardiovascular disease (hypertension and heart disease) stroke, hyperacidity.
- Wastage of time, effort, and energy.
- Loss of peace of mind.
- Poor self-control.
- Reduced interpersonal relationships.
- Temper tantrums and emotional outbursts.

TECHNIQUES TO CONTROL YOUR ANGRY THOUGHTS ARE AS FOLLOWS:

- Change your expectations–modifying your expectations can help you cope with anger.
- Develop more understanding–putting yourself in other person's shoes also help in understanding people.

TIPS FOR CONTROLLING ANGER

- imagery–just imagine without actually carrying out the action;
- thought stopping or cueing–switch over angry thoughts and concentrate on something you find enjoyable;
- various options for response are
  - directly express the anger;

- use humor;
- let go . . . Let it pass;
- divert your mind by focusing on something else;
- involve yourself in any physical activity;
- look at the situation in a different way;
- take time out to cool down; and
- learn and practice relaxation techniques.

ANGER MANAGEMENT TIPS FOR SELF-IMPROVEMENT

THE DO'S AND THE DONT'S

Develop empathy

- Empathy is a hallmark of emotional maturity.
- Empathy means the ability to understand the situation of others.
- The ability to empathize with others helps in controlling anger.

Develop tolerance and patience

- Impatience is a major reason why a person loses temper.
- Recognize that all problems cannot be resolved immediately.

Figure 3.3   Impatience causes loss of temper

When you start trying to control anger it may be difficult initially, but 'it is possible as a first step to at least reduce its frequency and intensity'.

Learn to analyze the situation neutrally without any emotional involvement. 'Rational thinking controls temper'.

Try to analyze and understand the origin of anger and what made you feel out of control and angry.

- This may make you understand that what you are feeling is 'displaced anger', for example when your boss insults you at office your unhappiness is expressed as extended anger toward family members.

- If you feel angry about a situation try to rectify it in a calm manner.
- Getting angry with a person is counterproductive.

Try to understand why anger was triggered both from your point of view and/or the other person who has got angry.

Try to sort out the matter on a one-to-one basis. Sort out your problems with the person you are angry with or who is angry with you directly rather than involving too many people.

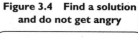

Figure 3.4   Find a solution and do not get angry

Figure 3.5   Two people discussing calmly

Remind yourself that you have one life with a limited life span and it is better spent in happiness and constructive actions than wasted in a negative emotion like anger.

When dealing with people and/or situations, learn to 'concentrate and emphasize the positive in others'.

Remember 'smile and the world smiles at you, cry and you cry alone'.

- If you greet someone with a smile and a nice hello, you will receive a nice response in return. If on the other hand, you respond with a frown on your face or approach someone with a grumpy face, it will hamper 'effective and positive communication' and you are likely to provoke anger in the other person.

Learn to trust others. Trust in others reduces trigger for anger.

THERE ARE VARIOUS METHODS THAT CAN CALM A PERSON

Figure 3.6 Diversion of attention helps reduce anger

- Learn to divert attention from your anger through massage therapy, gardening, physical exercise in any form—running, jogging, swimming, etc.

Music is very therapeutic in reducing anger

- Light music in the background can help in relaxation.

Figure 3.7 Singing and music helps in relaxing both the mind and the soul

Doing creative things calms your mind

Do something creative like:

Figure 3.8 Creative things help reduce negative feelings

- Painting or drawing.
- Making handicraft items or pottery.
- Knitting or embroidery.
- Write poems or stories.
- Cook a new dish.

Humor defuses anger

- Read, listen or tell jokes, or watch a cartoon or comedy when you are feeling angry.

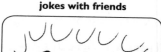

Figure 3.9   Share hilarious jokes with friends

THERE ARE SO MANY DIFFERENT WAYS OF TACKLING ANGER

- Each person will have to do a trial and error and choose a way that helps him best to calm down and control anger.

Develop your own anger management techniques

- For daily anger-provoking situations like gossiping, teasing, alcohol, road rage, frequently disagreeing with others, and stupid name-callings.

Count 10–100 before you speak out

- When you feel angry, counting is a good way to control angry words.
- Very often, this counting calms you down and you will not say the angry words you were about to blurt out.

Practice meditation

It helps in case one has an angry temperament. Meditation is known to have a calming effect and reduce the episodes of anger.

When you have a very stressful period ahead of you, plan short breaks for some 'personal time' so that you can de-stress yourself.

Figure 3.10   Meditation relieves anger

Get a partner to help you

- It could be your spouse, friend, relative or anyone whom you are close to and take his/her help to achieve the goals you set e.g., 'I will not get angry for a day', 'I will not fight for one week', 'I will not shout or yell for a month'.

LEARN VARIOUS ANGER MANAGEMENT TECHNIQUES

Learn progressive muscle relaxation. Progressive muscle relaxation involves tensing and relaxing various muscle groups. There is a five-point tension–relaxation cycle that you go through for each muscle group (Bernstein and Borkovec, 1973).

1. Focus: Focus attention on a particular muscle group.
2. Tense: Tense the muscle group.
3. Hold: Maintain the tension for five to seven seconds.
4. Release: Release the tension in the muscle group.
5. Relax: Spend 20–30 seconds focusing attention on the letting go of tension and further relaxing of the muscle group.

You can chant a mantra

Like 'OM' or 'Om Namai Shivaya'. Chanting of OM brings tranquility to mind.

You can also repeat words that can calm or relax you like 'relax' 'don't get upset' 'chill' and combine them with deep breathing till you feel you are in control of your emotions again.

Figure 3.11   Chanting mantra brings tranquillity to mind

'Role-playing' is also an effective anger management technique

Learn to understand your self-cues of impending anger

- For example, face getting hot, hands becoming cold or trembling, stammering of words.
- Immediately use the technique that helps you to prevent uncontrolled angry behavior.

When you are having heated arguments and you realize that you have reached your anger threshold, the best anger management is to stop and just walk away.

Figure 3.12   Walk out from an angry situation

Walk away when another person is shouting

When you are angry you should go away from that situation and 'sit alone quietly to calm down'.

Sitting in a garden or under a tree has a calming effect

Once you have calmed down and are able to think rationally you can go back into the situation again.

Expend your anger before you meet the person you are very angry with

- Imagine the person sitting in front of you and permit yourself to say all you wanted to. That will take away all your pain anger and resentment.
- You can also write an angry letter and tear it up after reading it once. This will unburden you so that when you actually meet the person you will be calm and collected, having already vented your anger.
- You can also do some physical exercise like jogging or swimming, or try some relaxation techniques, or listen to music before you go and face the person or situation.

Figure 3.13 Natural scenery relieves tension

When we are angry, we think we hear things that the other person never said. We also may not hear some of the things said as we are too angry to pay attention to the words. Listening in a calm fashion is very important to avoid misunderstandings. When you are angry you often say or do things, which you will later regret. In extreme anger you may commit a violent or unlawful act.

Hence do not confront someone when you are angry with him/her.

Go to a loved one or a friend whom you can trust to talk it over. They will calm you and may help you find an amicable solution.

Figure 3.14 Anger does not reduce by smoking or drinking

Don't indulge in alcohol or drugs when you are angry. It will only compound your anger and things will go out of hand.

At times anger keeps getting triggered by a particular situation or person. It then becomes important to take a break from the person or situation that is at home or office.

This break helps to diffuse the tension that has built up inside you and is creating anger. The break also helps you to analyze the situation more rationally. You can focus on the troublesome situation and not the person and find a rational solution.

Learn to be at peace with yourself

- Enjoy your own company.
- You do not have to be surrounded by people all the time.
- Being alone gives time for self-reflection, which leads to self-awareness and helps self-improvement.

Figure 3.15   Give yourself time for self-awareness

When you are feeling angry imagine how ferocious and ugly you look and imagine a loved one is watching you. How would they react to your negative image? It will help you to calm down.

A person who is very rigid and strict gets angry more easily.

- Learn to unwind and chill.
- Learn to laugh at yourself. This helps to release tension and angry feelings.

Figure 3.16   When angry look at your ugly face in the mirror

Look into the mirror when you are angry to see an unpleasant face

Improve your time management

- Don't set up unrealistic timetables and deadlines or procrastinate for self and others.
- You will always end up with 'too much to do in too little a time'.
- Such stress always triggers anger.

Figure 3.17   Good time management

**Figure 3.18   Take healthy food, do physical exercise,
and take proper sleep**

Practice a healthy lifestyle

Eat healthy, exercise, and have adequate sleep.

Take a nutritious diet and exercise daily. Lack of sleep causes sleep deficits and sleep deprivation syndrome that manifests as irritability and temper outbursts. So adequate sleep is necessary.

If you have a 'variety of interests in life with recreational outlets and warm relationships,' you will not find yourself getting angry often.

Find solutions in a cooperative and supportive manner rather than faultfinding, criticizing, and blaming. Negative emotions lead to anger, hostility, and aggression.

Learn to think and express positive emotions

Figure 3.19   Express positive emotions

- It is human to make mistakes.
- Learn to accept and recognize that YOU can be wrong and be the first to admit it.
- Many angry situations are dif-fused by an honest and sincere 'sorry'.
- You can always say sorry.

Forgiveness is also a tool for reducing anger, and increasing self-esteem and hopefulness toward one's future (Enright, 2002). It has been found that the trait, forgiveness is inversely related to aggressive driving, risky driving, and maladaptive form of driving anger expression; it is positively related to adaptive driving anger expression (Moore and Dahlen, 2008). Therefore forgiveness based treatments can be important strategies in reducing everyday risky, fast, and aggressive driving.

Act like a mature and responsible adult

Mace and Mace (1974) and Charney (1972) point out that anger is the greatest destroyer of marriages. Thus, instead of 'fighting' they recommend that you

- admit your anger;
- moderate or control it; and
- ask your partner for help in figuring out what two committed and caring people can do about the situation. Then work out an agreement.

Learn to ask for forgiveness and also learn to forgive

Figure 3.20   Forgiveness diffuses anger

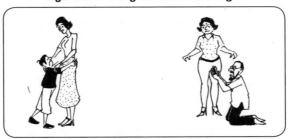

- Try to see the situation from the other person's perspective when you feel angry.
- Remember that everyone makes mistakes and it is only through mistakes that people learn how to improve.
- Find a role model. A person who has learnt to cope up with life is calm and happy in spite of adverse circumstances. Find out how he/she has managed. Adopt some of his/her ways that can help you.
- Remember what is in your hands is to change yourself and your responses to others, which may or may not change how others respond to you. Getting angry doesn't fix the situation and causes ill effects on you.

- When one commits some offense or error and feels remorse, there is no harm in apologizing. It has been found that receiving an apology can reduce self-reported aggression and improve the impression of the apologizer (Ohbuchi et al., 1989). A genuine apology is very effective in reducing anger (Holmes, 1990).

Body language is very powerful. Even if you control your words, other people can make impressions about your emotional state by negative body language.

If someone is offensive, you can learn to stand up for yourself without being aggressive.

- Without shouting and being loud, one can be assertive and tell others exactly what is bothering you about their behavior and that you will not accept it.

When you feel angry with someone instead of shouting, insulting, abusing, or sulking, learn to talk out your problem.

- Miscommunication causes more misunderstandings.
- If you both discuss things calmly, you may be able to find a resolution that does not involve an anger response.

It is better that you explain to the other person why you are feeling angry so that he/she can have an insight into your feelings and also will help in dealing with it effectively.

Unless you explain the cause of your anger, often the other person does not understand why you are angry and feels very hurt by your angry reactions, which according to them are not justified.

Never fight or argue with an angry person. Let the person 'cool down' and then discuss the situation rationally.

Avoid conflicts

- Before you say something inappropriate, think, is it going to solve the problem or is it going to escalate it?
- Do not lose your temper or fight while expressing criticism, disappointment, anger, or displeasure.

Figure 3.21   Never argue with an angry person

Tavris (1989) says the best thing, sometimes, to do about anger is nothing, including thinking nothing about the incident. The irritating event is mostly unimportant; its memory may soon fade away; if you stay quiet, the relationship stays civil and respectful.

When you are angry, adrenaline flows and increases your blood pressure, you have a lot of energy. Instead of using this 'natural high' to hurt others, you can use it in constructive ways. Examples: if a smart student in your class annoys you, use your anger-energy to study more and be a better competitor.

Don't lose your temper during discussions or arguments

Changing the way we think works very well. This is called cognitive reframing.

Try to replace your angry and irrational thoughts by more rational and calm thoughts.

Figure 3.22 Have calm discussions

- Anger management may include conceptual reframing or cognitive restructuring, identifying triggering stimuli, and relaxation training which includes reducing physical state of tension so that anger does not lead to aggression.

'Use statements that express your feelings rather than statements that put blame on others.'

- For example, say 'I feel upset when you keep your room in a mess as I get tired cleaning it', rather than 'you are very messy or you always keep your room messy'.

Accept that everyone cannot like you just as you cannot like everyone you meet.

- If you do not insist on having approval of all the people around you, you will not feel disappointed and angry if some people don't like you.

Live by Gandhi's non-violence philosophy and Carl Roger's approach of 'unconditional positive regard' for everyone.

A TO Z TIPS FOR ANGER MANAGEMENT

Figure 3.23

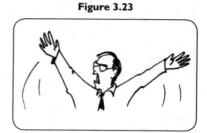

Alert yourself to the first sign of anger, so that you can control before it gets out of hand.

Figure 3.24

Aim at keeping a peaceful atmosphere at home and work.

Figure 3.25

Believe in the goodness of human beings. It makes you less angry.

Figure 3.26

Channelize your thoughts in keeping calm when you start getting angry.

Figure 3.27

'**Diffuse anger** at the earliest stage' so that it does not escalate and get out of control.

Figure 3.28

Enlighten and **empower** yourself on anger control.

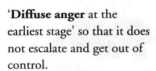

Figure 3.29

Empathize—Keep your
heart open at all times.

Figure 3.30

Educate yourself on anger
management.

Figure 3.31

Friendship helps to control
your anger.

Figure 3.32

Get support from people who love you, to help you control anger.

Figure 3.33

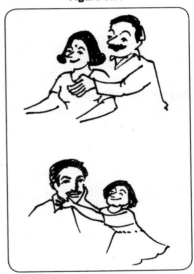

Happiness drives away anger. Maintain a happy and calm atmosphere.

Figure 3.34

Initiate conflict resolution when there is an angry situation.

Figure 3.35

Joy should be all around when you deal with people.

Figure 3.36

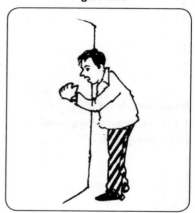

Key to anger management is tolerance to imperfections that are not vital.

Figure 3.37

Love yourself and others around you.

Figure 3.38

Listen to the person who is angry with you. You will understand if you are at fault.

Figure 3.39

Learn from your past mistakes . . . when you got angry last time what were the negative repercussions.

Figure 3.40

Learn to accept what cannot be changed.

Figure 3.41

Let go of what is beyond your control.

Figure 3.42

Motivate others with compassion.

Figure 3.43

Mistakes of others should be forgiven and forgotten.

Figure 3.44

Never use the word 'never' . . . this is a word that closes all negotiations.

Figure 3.45

Observe . . . the other person's body language, which often reveals more than the words that are being said.

Figure 3.46

Orient yourself to the viewpoint of others also.

Figure 3.47

Practice what you preach.
Question yourself whether
you are expressing anger in
the right way.

Figure 3.48

Remember your own
childhood when dealing with
children or your own past
mistakes when dealing with
adults and be more forgiving.

Figure 3.49

Don't let anger 'simmer',
it harms you mentally and
physically.

Figure 3.50

Take time to explain things rather than lose your temper.

Figure 3.51

Unearth the good in every person you meet.
Value everyone's feelings and needs.

Figure 3.52

Verify facts before you jump to wrong conclusions. Clarify information.

Figure 3.53

Don't vilify others specially without knowing facts.

Figure 3.54

Welcome mistakes as learning opportunities.

Figure 3.55

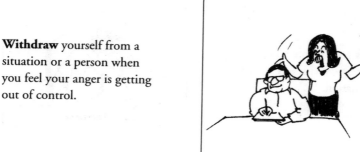

Withdraw yourself from a situation or a person when you feel your anger is getting out of control.

Figure 3.56

Xmas spirit should be
practiced all year around.
You are the best person to
decide how the world is going
to be for you.

Figure 3.57

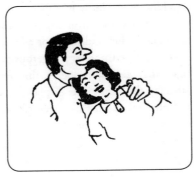

Zero down to foster loving
relationships.

ANGER MANAGEMENT IN FAMILY

> '*There is nothing either good or bad but thinking makes it so.*'
> —*William Shakespeare*

Anger is the most commonly occurring negative emotion in a family, which
develops between parents, among children, and between parents and children.
It is a major cause of fights and unhappiness in families. Anger experts say
that anger develops more often in a family environment—between married
partners and with children—than in any other human relationship. When anger
turns violent, it results in emotional and physical abuse of our loved one.

Figure 3.58   Anger in family

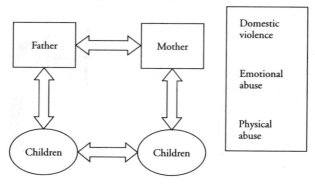

Children learn about anger, anger expression, and anger management by watching their family members, others in their community, and people at school. If they come from a harsh home environment, where anger is managed through alcohol and drugs or abuse, they begin to learn that experiencing anger can be either very dangerous or very powerful. Those who act out the anger may destroy property, threaten others, and even show disrespect to others in the family. The display of anger is often associated with emotional and physical assaults like yelling, screaming, slapping, hitting an object, or self-injurious behavior. If anger is turned inward, which is often done with females, it also has negative consequenes. They become withdrawn and suffer from feelings of hopelessness and despair.

PARENT–CHILD ANGER

It is extremely important that parents need to state clear rules, praise good behavior, and consistently punish violations.

- Parents who have an inept discipline style, threaten, nag, and constantly scold the child.
- Such parents use a great deal of punishment to counter the child's response with anger.
- This pattern of behavior has been repeatedly linked to children's aggressiveness in elementary school.

Effective parental anger management is required to control disruptive behavior among children.

Hence anger management and learning a healthy way of expressing anger is necessary to keep mental equilibirium and happiness.

Staying in a family means a loving, supportive, and secure environment

Figure 3.59 A happy loving family

- Families are one of the most prominent and supportive groups in any culture.
- Parents can provide an environment of love and encouragement as well as positive arenas for anger and aggression.
- If children are raised in safe and loving homes with a strong, loving relationship with a parent/another adult they feel safe and secure, and develop a sense of trust.
- Thus parents play an important role in reducing aggression and violence by developing safety and security for the children while they are growing up and also when they are grown up.
- Studies all over the world have shown that such children are less likely to develop behavioral problems in their lives.
- It has been seen that children with warm and affectionate relationships with parents develop the ability to maintain successful marriages, social friendships, and relationships with their own children (Franz et al., 1991).
- Hence parents must make efforts to have positive, warm, and affectionate relationships with their children.
- Nowadays, with the changing socialization practices, families structure is getting negatively affected in a number of ways.
- The size of a family is shrinking as more double income and nuclear families are coming up.
- Due to increased professional responsibilities and other problems such as differential views of parents, marital discord, there is inappropriate communication between elders and children.

More and more, families are becoming 'disturbed or dysfunctional families'. 'Adequate parental training is very much required for healthy development of the child.'

SOME OF THE IMPORTANT ANGER MANAGEMENT TIPS FOR FAMILY

Children learn to express a lot of emotions by imitation. Therefore, parents should learn to express their angry feelings in non-aggressive ways.

- When adults show a lot of anger children are confused. Children have an impaired ability to understand and relate to emotions in the background of anger.
- Parents should not impose excessive demands on children. Excessive demands can ruin their independence and ability, which can make them more depressed and irritated, which can result in anger and aggression.

Children, especially as they get older, should have a say in making decisions related to their life.

- Parents should not force their goals on children and show anger and frustration when they are not met with. Goals set by the individual himself are more likely to be achieved instead of ones that have been imposed upon them. Therefore, children should be encouraged to think and take decisions according to their interests and capabilities.
- Working parents have to be even more careful about their parental style and anger management behavior. Children of working parents are likely to develop some deviant behaviors because they may not get proper parental attention and guidance in everyday problems. Therefore, time management on the part of the parents should be promoted so that they don't ignore the child's well-being due to their work.

Parental training about child development is required, especially so in double-income nuclear families for helping children in becoming self-confident, skilled in solving their own problems, and having an adequate self-concept.

- Many children express their feelings by kicking, screaming, swearing, hitting or throwing things because they don't know other ways to express their angry feelings that can get parental attention. Therefore, parents must learn to respond to initial signs of deviance that the child show and respond in a positive manner, before the irritation worsens and relatively permanent inadequate behavioral patterns are formed.

- Children must be encouraged to voice their opinion sensibly and logically rather than resorting to temper tantrums, hitting each other, etc. Parents must teach children by their own example how to express negative feelings in a constructive and healthy way that will elicit a positive and helpful response.

Learn to say I am angry and discuss instead of getting out of control

It is a good habit to learn to say, 'I am angry' or 'I feel very angry about this' and discuss issues, rather than show anger by verbal abuse, physical assault, temper tantrums, etc.

Figure 3.60 Accept your anger and feel sorry for that

- Teach your children how to respond appropriately when others use insults or threats or deal with anger by hitting. Explain that these are inappropriate behaviors. Empower children to control their own behavior by teaching them to regulate their emotions and impulses.
- Keep your child away from people who get easily aggressive. Encourage your child to avoid friendship and company of such people if they cannot be persuaded to change their behavior.
- Learn from your child, enjoy them, value them, guide them, and allow them to be themselves. Live life in the true sense.

Family members must ensure that sons and daughters are praised equally for equal achievement. Gender discrimination and bias toward either gender can harbor resentment and animosity, leading to chronic anger and aggression.

Figure 3.61 Don't discriminate between your son and daughter

Compassionate parenting

- Regularly practice compassionate parenting. It helps in reducing anger, hostility, and aggression in children and parents. Build loving relationships as they provide freedom from resentment and emotional constraints.

- Be nice to your kids and they will be nice to you and to everyone else.
- Avoid teaching, correcting, or instructing when the other person or child is angry.

You can practice the habit of not reacting to your child's anger or anger of any other family member by not talking to him/her, till they have calmed down.

- But don't use this as a punishment. Don't leave the loved one alone by ignoring for much longer than an hour or two.

Learn to analyze what provokes your anger

As a parent, your anger might be triggered toward children when they are messy, don't cooperate, or disobey your wishes.

- Discuss with your children why they feel angry. Their anger might be triggered when someone ignores the good things they do, puts them down, or shows disrespect for their acts. Therefore, analyzing what triggers anger is the first step toward learning how to control it.

Even if you always feel angry, use clear, respectful, and nonaggressive language to make your feelings known. The tone of voice you use is also very important. You can use all the right words but if they're laced with anger, you're going to end up in a hostile, unhealthy fight.

Don't be harsh when you are angry. It hurts the other person.

Figure 3.62 Harsh parenting

- Much stress in a family can be reduced by clarifying family members' roles and responsibilities. Make sure everyone understands clearly what is expected of him or her. Communicate positively and discuss issues openly and clarify responsibility.
- Role-playing is also an effective anger management technique. It helps a person to control personal conflicts, and it generates options that lead to resolution.

- Well-presented stories about anger and other emotions can validate children's feelings and give information about anger.
- Supervised play with toys can be very effective in helping children release anger.
- Practice reflective listening and let the child know he/she is being heard.
- Most children cannot accept their shortcomings and accept situations. Parents should teach children to enjoy living and accept themselves as they are.

When children accept their shortcomings, they will not have intense, internal conflicts, which are the major causes of several problems. Optimism should always be encouraged and pessimism should be discouraged.

- Values of kindness, love, care, honesty, and responsibility should be inculcated right from childhood. These characteristics help in developing self-confidence, courage, and inner strength that may later help in solving conflicting situations.
- Values of respect, pride, and heritage can be important sources of strength in children, especially if they are confronted with negative peer pressure, live in a violent neighborhood, or attend a rough school. Therefore, these values should be fostered in the family to make children emotionally strong in dealing with these problems.
- Children should learn some habits of caring for others and hence be encouraged to join some community organizations/institutions to do social work.
- Many children do not indulge in activities as failures and criticism give rise to feeling of guilt and frustration. Enthusiasm and appreciation should be encouraged positively, instead of criticism about failures.

Encourage children to come to you when they feel tense or face problems. Feelings of nightmare, irrational thoughts, and phobias should be openly discussed specially in young children.

Figure 3.63 Show empathy

Have open communication with your children

- Express empathy and understanding by imagining yourself in the position of the child and attempting to see things from his/her viewpoint. Put yourself in the other person's shoes. Emphasize that loved ones, usually don't set out to annoy but to help us.

- Take help of a family member or friend to control anger. Set up goals such as 'I will not get angry for one day', 'I will not fight for one week', 'I will not yell for two weeks'. It always helps to have someone monitor your goals.
- If you feel injustice has been done to you do not keep cribbing and boiling with resentment. Learn to be assertive and get your due, without violence and anger. You will act as a model for your child to follow.

Avoid the negative and irritating words 'never, ever, and always.'

- Resist taunting and humiliating the other person when you are angry, especially in public.
- If children or adults are constantly under work pressure, it triggers anger very easily. Learn to build recreational activities in your day-to-day activities. It helps to keep things happy and calm.
- Make your child understand that revenge and resentments are futile and forgiving and forgetting has a 'liberating effect' on the mind. Practice forgiving and forgetting yourself to act as a role model.

Get the children's opinion

Childern often are angry and frustrated because they constantly receive instructions from everyone around them, at home, in school, everyone is always telling them what to do.

Figure 3.64   Respect your children's opinion

- Try another approach. Get their opinions on what they would like to do and guide them accordingly. If they feel they are doing what they are interested in and what they want (which is often the right thing) they will be happy and cooperative.

Get help if anger gets unmanageable

If you find that your anger or the anger in your family or work setup is getting very diffcult to cope up with, seek help.

- Get consultation from a professional or set up a community or parental support group.
- Discussing with other parents and adults who have dealt with the same kind of situations can be very useful.
- The best advice often can be given by another person who has experience in successfully dealing with angry children or another family member or friend.

ANGER MANAGEMENT IN SCHOOLS

Many schools have become battlegrounds between students and teachers. The print and electronic media are filled with the reports of unrests and interpersonal disputes among students, between student and teachers, and among teachers themselves.

In today's fast paced and competitive society, schools with latest technological advancement are focused on raising students' academic standards.

- School administration, teachers, and parents are more concerned in getting good academic results above all other issues.
- The purpose of teaching has become reading, writing, and solving problems.
- We are bringing out good technicians, engineers, management professionals, and doctors, but no one is thinking

Figure 3.65   Teachers should focus on the overall development of their students

of the stress we are subjecting them to and the mental health of these children.

It has been well documented that emotional intelligence (EQ) is as important in life as the Intelligence Quotient (IQ) for success and happiness in life. Children are put in coaching classes for academics, sports, and in other classes to pursue their artistic talents, but no one sends his children for managing their emotions.

- Art of living, meditation, and stress management classes have become very popular for high level executives. If children are trained in such classes when they are young, they will grow up to be mentally competent and balanced adults who do not need such classes.
- Along with raising academic standards, it is also necessary to instill lifestyle behaviors, values, and harmony, to assist our children to contribute in a positive form to our society and to the whole world.

Stress leads to anger and hostility and we have an ever-increasing incidence of 'life style related disorders' like diabetes, high blood pressure, cardiac disease, and strokes in young adult world over, but more specifically in India.

- Management professionals are becoming more aggressive and violent. Professionals with polluted minds are very dangerous to our society.

Those days are gone when school had been one of the safest havens for our children and children sitting quietly would wait for the teacher.

- Nowadays, fighting, bullying, teasing, name-calling, pushing, hitting, beating, assaults, and sexual harassment have become frequently occurring activities in many schools, harassing both boys and girls.
- This results in the AHA-syndrome (anger, hostility, and aggression) and has negative effects on the physiology, psychology, and social interactions of growing children and adolescents.

Many students choose to avoid harassment by either skipping school, or dropping out of a particular activity like sport, or in extreme cases, dropping out of school.

- Because of poor communication many parents do not realize why their children are avoiding school or various sports and extracurricular activities. This results in their nagging or scolding the child.

- Thus the children come under pressure, both at home and school and as a result develop disruptive behavior.
- As a result of hostile interactions and angry reactions, aggressive children tend to be rejected by their peers. This peer rejection, in turn, fosters more aggression and inappropriate behavior.

Reducing anger among school children is not a simple task. Harsh punishment procedures or corporal punishment can harm a student's physical and psychological well-being and cause scars that may last for life.

- Special training of teachers is extremely important for implementing effective classroom management strategies that reduce anger and aggressive behavior in students and enhance social and academic competence.
- The failure of schools and teachers to take necessary action in controlling anger problems at school has lead to many serious consequences, including aggression, violence, shooting, rape, and even murder.
- Teachers must be aware of possible 'gang' activity within the school. They must set the parameter of normal behavior in the campus.
- When teachers note adverse change in the behavior of students, they must call their parents.

Studies have shown that greatest increase in crime and inappropriate behavior is occurring at the elementary school level (Goldstein et al., 1999; Dahlberg, 1998). Now the question arises, from where such behavior arises and what we should do about it?

- Goldstein (1999) indicates that disruptive and aggressive behavior is learned from a child's total environment.
- Anger is one of the most powerful emotions experienced by children.
- Children often have difficulties in expressing feelings and controlling their impulses.
- They continue to allow their anger to get control of them instead of effective anger management.
- Effective anger control programs are needed to manage anger on part of both teachers and students, before it leads to serious problems.

SOME IMPORTANT ANGER MANAGEMENT TIPS IN SCHOOLS FOR TEACHERS AS WELL AS FOR STUDENTS

- Teacher must be kind and gentle with their words and actions, and show respect to others. They should become a role model for students to follow, so that they are also gentle and respectful toward peers.

Teachers should create an environment that enables effective teaching and learning. Satisfied and happy students means less anger in the school.

Figure 3.66 Teachers should be role models for their students

- Giving short breaks in schools are very necessary for the development of a child.
- In the recess time children get an oppurtnity to interact, use language and nonverbal communications, make decisions, solve problems, and deal with emotional trials.
- Due to academic pressure many schools are cutting down on recess timing. Many feel recess should be avoided to prevent interactions among children that can lead to problems.
- There should be well-planned recreational activities in school.
- Healthy reading material should be encouraged for development of creativity and other cognitive abilities of children.

Figure 3.67 Teachers should create a happy environment in classrooms

- Parents and teachers need to work together to develop such habits in children.

Moral education as part of curriculum

Moral education was an important part of school curriculm in the past. Many schools today do not give enough emphasis on this. Moral science classes are skipped or taken very lightly by students.

- Early school experiences are very important to provide a base for the moral development of children.

All-round development should be the focus

Schools should not focus only on academic success but efforts should be made to ensure an all-round development of children.

- In order to encourage and boost social responsibility and positive attitude in the students, the school should have prizes for social service or any noble activiity done by students. Recognition and praise of such students will encourage more students to adopt such behaviors.
- Research has shown that youth who belong to a socially appropriate group sponsored and supported by the school (e.g., academic club or social organization) are less likely to demonstrate aggression and violence (Catalano et al., 1999).
- Therefore the school should have facilities to conduct activities for such and organizations and children should be encouraged to join them. Recognizing and rewarding the good work done in this field will encourage more student participation.

Figure 3.68 Children should have a playground for recreation

Anger management is a must for teachers and parents

Anger management program is very necessary not only for students but also for teachers and parents. Such efforts are much more likely to be successful if parents and teachers model themselves with the appropriate skills and reward responsible behavior in their children.

- Physical punishment may produce obedience for a short period, but continued over time, tends to increase the probability of aggressive and violent behavior among children.
- Therefore, both teachers and parents should avoid physical punishments and make use of other implicit ways of tackling problems of children.

Corporal punishment should be avoided

Children who do not do well academically or in extra curricular activities often feel depressed, frustrated, and angry and these result in aggressive behavior. School should have programs that can handle such problems of children's poor academic performance and under-achievement.

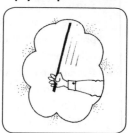

Figure 3.69 Avoid physical punishment

- They can be made to divert their potential to other fields where they can utilize their potential effectively.
- Unfavorable school environment can lead to anger, frustration, and aggression in children, e.g., school atmosphere becomes unhealthy with less personal space, congested, poorly ventilated, dark and dirty rooms, unplanned design of school building, lack of play facilities.
- A teacher can demoralize students by playing 'favorites'. Teachers must not carry their internal politics, vices, and prejudices to the classrooms.

Therefore, a healthy inter-personal environment must be fostered in educational institutions.

- Students often become the target of politics played by teachers. A sense of injustice fosters chronic anger in students that can result in violence.
- Teachers should learn to make use of various behavior techniques such as satiation, time-out, and over-correction for adequately dealing with students' anger and aggressive behavior.

Violence against teachers should be punished

Teachers must maintain a high profile in terms of behavioral expectations of students. Violence against teachers should be punished strongly and such students may be debarred to set an example in the school so that others will not dare to repeat such actions.

Figure 3.70   A student threatening a teacher with a knife

- Between 1995 and 1999, in the United States, teachers were victims of 342,000 nonfatal crimes per year.
- In 1994, 12 percent of all elementary and secondary school teachers were threatened with injury by a student from their school (Kaufman et al., 2001).
- Parents should be clearly informed that violence in any form is not acceptable in school.

A counselor or school psychologist should be present in every school to help children in resolving their conflicts and to curb any deviation in the behaviors.

- Teachers must establish a good rapport with students and develop means to know students' needs, progress and successes on a regular basis. This reduces anger on both sides.
- Children need to be taught social skills to make and keep friends by sharing, giving compliments, and working cooperatively. This reduces unnecessary manifestations of anger.

Very often parents and teachers get angry with children for disobedience. Many young children do not understand or comprehend instructions. It is important for adults to clarify word meanings and give clear instructions. It is necessary to ascertain that children have understood and not assume that they have.

- Children should be encouraged to vent out their angry feelings in some meaningful ways like discussion, or other constructive activities, rather than taking recourses to temper tantrums.
- Just as bad behavior should be punished, good behavior needs be rewarded. Reinforced behavior may also contribute in promoting values and norms in children.

- Children who have learnt unlawful ways of expressing anger are likely to revert to their old style, even after undergoing anger management training (Miller and Sperry, 1987). Teachers need to be constantly vigilant and monitor such children by giving support when needed.

There are many well-proved modalities that control anger and aggression. Spirituality (Yoga, meditation) promotes self-confidence, self-esteem, and courage in difficult times.

- It has been found that children with some spiritual background are less likely to engage in aggressive and violent acts.
- Therefore there should be classes for these and such values should be nurtured in the school.

ANGER MANAGEMENT AT WORKPLACE

'The mind is its own place, and in itself can make a heaven of hell a hell of heaven.'
—John Milton

Stress and overload at work, excess responsibility, late working hours, making way through daily traffic jams, etc., are common scenarios working men and women have to face. If you cannot cope up with your anger at these day-to-day stressors at work, a job can be a most unpleasant experience. Studies show that one out of four American workers is chronically angry at work (Gibson and Barsade, 1999), contributing to more than 16,000 threats and 700 attacks in offices across the United States each work day (Kaufer and Mattman, 2004).

The most common causes of anger at workplace are

- delay and absenteeism of both co-workers and employees;
- inefficiency, slacking, intentional poor work, pilfering, or stealing;
- unnecessary arguments, and hostility.

Many people hold a grudge against various people in the office, which can reduce job performance as well as job satisfaction.

Some anger management tips

These tips can help you to control your anger at workplace and to make your work environment more pleasant and happy.

- Always remember that everyone is likely to make a mistake, including you and hence avoid saying unkind words to others.
- It should be remembered that if you distrust people and feel they are out to provoke you then you might be getting unnecessarily and unjustifiably angry with others.
- When you feel angry with someone, first find out whether the other person has made a genuine mistake. Don't assume they want to trouble you.
- If you want harmonious working atmosphere, learn to develop good interpersonal relationships with your colleagues so that when there are problematic situations, communication channels are always open.
- Many times there are conflicts due to miscommunication. They are better solved by calm, one to one discussion. Angry reactions will only escalate matters.
- When you get angry take time to cool down before you take any action. Decision taken when angry can be a wrong one and that can have long-term negative implications and also affect your job.
- Always confront persons on a one-to-one basis. Talking through a third person often creates misunderstandings.
- Avoid unnecessary arguments with colleagues and seniors. It gives rise to a hostile atmosphere that is not pleasant to work in.
- If you are in a meeting and you feel anger building up, take a break that will give you a change of atmosphere and help you to calm down. Take a cup of coffee/tea, have a snack as often since hunger triggers anger. Do some fun thing on the computer, doodle, or draw some cartoons. Use whatever method that works best with you to calm down and be in control.
- Practice active listening.
- Focus your attention on the major work on hand. Learn to avoid irritation by ignoring minor unimportant things.
- If you are angry with someone or someone is angry with you, approach him/her saying 'let us talk it over and find a solution', instead of fighting.
- Feeling of anger also decreases among people who had walked through a nature reserve but increased among people who had walked in an urban setting without vegetation (Hartig et al., 2003).

Time management is of essence

If you have good time management skill and you are able to deliver the work assigned to you in the proper time frame:

- People will respect you and react to you positively.
- You also will get a reputation of being reliable, committed, sincere, and dependable.

Good time management is extremely important in life if you want to reduce your own stress and the stress that you give to others.

Figure 3.71   Learn time management to avoid unnecessary stress

- You will generate a lot of anger against you and people will not be happy working with you.
- You will not be acceptable as a team member as you will be given a label of a person who does not keep commitment and is not reliable.
- If you are trying to unsuccessfully meet deadlines all the time, you are going to be stressed out. This will mean you would be irritable, short-tempered, and not a pleasant person to work with and hence you will generate more anger.

Hence always do proper time management for each assignment.

Learn to be forgiving and don't holds grudges, which result in chronic anger and resentment

- Many people get angry because they have set certain standards, which they expect others to follow. Remember all individuals have their own ideas and cannot behave the way you want them to behave.
- When there is a conflict, instead of getting angry and reacting, think what can I do to stop this conflict and you will find a solution.
- It is important to learn various skills like interpersonal relationships, communication skills, negotiation skills, if you want to get along harmoniously with your colleagues, subordinates, and your superiors.
- Develop self-awareness. Always understand what your capabilities are and what your limitations are. Set your goals according to your capabilities and accept work that is within your capacity.

Anger and criticism

Always accept criticism positively.

- Then people will be happy to give you a feedback which will help you to improve further.

If you get angry on receiving a negative feedback

- people will never tell you the truth and you will continue living in a fool's paradise.

On the other hand, if you understand that someone is always criticizing you because they are jealous and just want to put you down

- learn to ignore it and not waste your time and get angry;
- this only gives them unnecessary importance and your anger makes them happy;
- don't fall into this trap.

When you give someone a negative feedback

- learn to use constructive language;
- if you taunt or criticize, they will get on the defensive and react with anger.

It is good to be ambitious but not over ambitious. Setting goals beyond your capacity leads to frustration and then jealousy and envy about others who are going higher than you. It also brings out negative traits like back biting, maligning, which will further cause people to get angry with you.

Figure 3.72 Set realistic goals to avoid frustration that leads to anger

Learn to identify what makes you repeatedly angry in your workplace. Is your trigger a person, a situation, or a particular assignment? Once you have identified your triggers, try to avoid them. If that is not possible, find solutions to overcome your negative reaction. In case that is not possible, use anger management techniques to control your anger.

- When you feel you are getting angry, learn to control your anger before it escalates and goes out of control and you do rash things which you will regret later. Use the calming and anger control techniques described under self-anger management tips.
- Remember that just because someone is trying to provoke you or insult you does not mean you have to retaliate or react. Always be in control of the situation and your emotions. Learn to respond in a more controlled manner.
- A person who gets angry very quickly needs to work a lot on anger management by proper counseling and anger management training. Often a person is not angry by temperament but may get angry under certain situations.
- Poor diet and lack of proper sleep and no exercise makes a person more irritable and quick to get angry. Learn to maintain a healthy balanced lifestyle.
- Take help of someone to control your anger in your office. Talking out with this person when you are angry will help you to calm down and handle the situation rationally.

There is a difference between being aggressive and assertive. Aggression involves anger and violence and provokes hostility.

- Being assertive means standing up for your rights in a firm and appropriate way with calmness, while also being aware of the rights and needs of others.
- Assertiveness does not involve any aggression verbally, psychologically, or physically.

One has to make clear compartments between home and workplace. One should not bring stress of work to home and vice versa. It leads to angry out-bursts, both with co-workers and family members. One has to strike a balance between work and family.

Sleep deficit and sleep deprivation

If you have late nights every day, you get what is called sleep deficit. Sleep deficit accumulates over time if one does not sleep properly and leads to sleep deprivation syndrome which has symptoms like:

Figure 3.73   Chronic late nights will lead to sleep deprivation and sleep deficit

- headaches, high blood pressure;
- feelings of fatigue and tiredness, inability to concentrate, hyperacidity, body ache, and various aches and pains.

One of the major manifestations of the same is anger and irritability. If you have some late nights you must make up with sleeping for more hours next day or at weekend, to avoid sleep deprivation.

- There are times when you are constantly on the edge due to some work pressure or deadlines in office or some domestic problems at home. This means you are constantly losing your temper and yelling and shouting at somebody and landing into fights all the time.

Figure 3.74   Talk over issues that are making you angry

- If you are not clear about how to handle a situation talking over the issue with someone you love at home or a close friend can be very helpful.

- If you feel your work pressure is getting out of hand, confide in your boss, take help from colleagues but don't let your anger harm your work or assignment that can jeopardize your career.
- Don't be a workaholic. Balance work with recreation. Give time to your family. This will help you unwind and keep your family happy, giving rise to a peaceful atmosphere at home.
- Change your pattern of thinking. Are you being given more work by your boss because he wants to harass you or you are being overloaded because you are extremely capable and able to handle crisis.
- Viewing people or situations more realistically and less personally can prevent you from being angry in the first place.

If you are going to a meeting or meeting a person for an issue, where you know you are likely to lose your temper, do some homework at home—practice your responses.

- You can do this by writing out various scenarios where you can decide beforehand how you will respond to the various comments and answers you will get from the person you are anticipating trouble.

Figure 3.75   Practice your responses

- You can also act out in front of a mirror. This has an additional advantage of you observing your body language, which is as important as verbal communication.
- You may find these techniques ridiculous, funny, or embarrassing at first, but gradually you will realize the advantage that you are getting by such techniques.
- There are no surprises, you are in control of whatever situation that may arise and instead of reacting in a rash and impulsive manner, you are responding in a controlled and rational manner.

THERAPEUTIC INTERVENTION FOR MANAGEMENT OF ANGER

Anger is basic to human existence. We need to understand anger in order to learn to use it constructively for the enhancement of life, and not allow it to cause the destruction of life. Angry people consistently display deficiencies in interpersonal skills, planning, and in anger management. Anger often leads to aggression. Aggressive people are skilled in intimidating, harassing, manipulating, and fighting.

Anger causes harm both to the person who gets angry and the person who bears the brunt of the anger. Anger related issues cause loss of happiness, peace, and harmony at home, community, and workplace. Hence anger is one negative emotion that needs control and management.

In the first three parts of this section we emphasized on some important anger management tips that can be used in family, school, and workplace scenarios. These tips are very effective for the layman in dealing with everyday anger, hostility, and aggression. One can be cool and control his/her anger by following these simple tips.

If you find that in spite of trying out various techniques you are still unable to master your anger, then there is an urgent need of taking professional help.

In the present part, we are discussing some empirically proved anger management techniques, intervention programs, and other anger reducing strategies that have been proved clinically in anger management in various settings and can be taken from the experts in their areas.

Don't regard taking professional help as a stigma, get help in the right time.

Figure 3.76   Take professional help

People with problem of anger should not hesitate to consider getting counseling or taking therapeutic intervention for anger management. This is not a stigma but self preservation, as uncontrolled anger can harm you and your life. Anger hampers many areas of functioning and leads to physical aggression, domestic violence, alcohol and drug abuse, and road rage. Anger also causes negative health consequences like high blood pressure, coronary heart disease, stroke, cancer.

Some of the most empirically supported interventions are

- cognitive-behavioral interventions including relaxation,
- coping skills,

- cognitive interventions,
- behavioral coping and social skills training, and
- problem-solving skills training.

COGNITIVE-BEHAVIORAL INTERVENTION

This involves various methods that try to change the thoughts and behavior response of people to various situations and the most commonly used intervention is by cognitive-behavioral therapy (CBT). It is based on learning theory and information processing models that involve the use of relaxation, reappraisal of events, coping skills such as imagery and distraction, and interpersonal or social skills training that are later rehearsed in anger-provoking situations, followed by contingent reinforcement (Beck and Farnandez, 1998). CBT has been proved very effective to change the thoughts and behavioral response of people in various situations, particularly in clinical sample (Deffenbacher et al., 2002).

Cognitive behavioral approach

This is a mode of treatment that has been found to be very useful in patients who have emotional distress, including anger problems. Cognitive approaches assume that 'what determines whether a person will get angry in a particular situation' depends upon a person's

- individual perceptions;
- individual expectations; and
- individual appraisal of the situations.

The aim of cognitive treatments is to modify the 'cognition' or the thinking and response of a person, so that given the same situation the person

- either will not experience anger, or
- the intensity of the anger will remain at a level that does not interfere with adaptive behavior.

The key components of cognitive-behavioral approach are as follows:

- Educating the client/patient about anger, stress, and aggression.
- Teaching them to self-monitor their anger frequency, intensity, and situational triggers.

- Helping them to construct a personal anger provocation hierarchy. This is to be created from the self-monitoring data, which is also used for practicing and testing coping skills.
- Helping them to reduce their excessive and quick arousal by various techniques like progressive muscle relaxation, breathing focused relaxation, and guided imagery training.
- Helping in cognitive restructuring by altering their focus of attention, modifying their appraisals, and using self-instructions.
- Training them in behavioral coping skills in communication and respectful assertiveness which is modeled and rehearsed with a therapist.
- Practicing the cognitive, arousal regulatory, and behavior-coping skills while visualizing and role-playing intense anger-arousing scenes from the personal hierarchies, progressively.

COGNITIVE RESTRUCTURING AND SELF-INSTRUCTIONAL TRAINING

Cognitive restructuring is a method by which a angry person is trained to

- replace 'hot' anger-related cognitions with 'cooler' more calming thoughts.

Similarly, self-instructional training is a program that encourages angry persons to modify their verbal self-talk e.g.,

- 'There is no point getting mad right now' or
- 'Instead of getting angry, I am going to deal with this constructively'.

The effectiveness of the above programs for anger management has been well documented in studies of community volunteers (Novaco, 1975; Tafrate and Kassinove, 1998; Hazaleus and Deffenbacher, 1986; Moon and Eisler, 1983).

SYSTEMATIC DESENSITIZATION

Systematic desensitization techniques were developed for the reduction of conditioned anxiety reactions. This helped to condition a response, which prevents anxiety from occurring in the presence of anxiety-evoking situation.

- Deep muscle relaxation has been found to be the best anxiety reducing method.
- Once the person is relaxed, items of anxiety-provoking stimuli are presented either in words or imaginary techniques.
- This leads to a systematic desensitization and it is seen that anger and aggression can be modified by developing incompatible responses to provoking situations.

AROUSAL REDUCTION

Most people who get angry quickly or lose their temper at the slightest provocation have a very high arousal behavior. Arousal reduction procedures begin with helping the person to identify signs of arousal, including its intensity, duration, and liability, as well as latency in reactivity.

- Reduction of arousal involves regulation of breathing, which is the central rhythm of the body.
- Slow and deep breathing is demonstrated and induced in each session, and clients are encouraged to practice on their own (Novaco, 2006).

PROBLEM-SOLVING TREATMENT

For those persons who have deficits in their ability to guide their behavior in an appropriate manner, problem-solving approaches are employed. These have shown good results in studies on angry college students (Moon and Eislser, 1983) and adult parents, who had either committed child abuse or were identified as being at risk to do so (Whitman et al., 1987).
These approaches are likely to be most helpful for those persons

- who do not exhibit behavioral skill deficits (e.g., poor social skills) but lack general problem-solving skills by which one can assess angering situations and learn to select from among various behavioral coping skills, they are already good at (Deffenbecher, 1995).

Problem-solving intervention helps to reduce anger by helping the person to develop cognitive strategies for

- approaching and defining anger provoking events as 'problems' and
- then generating, evaluating, and implementing solutions to the 'problem' in a calm and reasonable manner.

BEHAVIORAL COPING/SOCIAL SKILLS TRAINING

Behavioral coping and social skills interventions target the manner in which anger is expressed. There are several coping skills that may be relevant to anger management, e.g.,

- Parenting, financial planning, assertiveness.
- These depend upon the source of provocation and the nature of skill deficits (Dahlen and Deffenbacher, 2001).

Social skills training teach clients appropriate skills for handling anger in social situations. An important assumption of this approach is that anger-prone individuals have social skill deficits that result in their inability to resolve social anger-provoking situations.

There are various methods used to teach social skills.

- Discussion, modeling, rehearsal, and feedback for teaching behaviors believed to contribute to pro-social engagement and for teaching general interpersonal skills (Deffenbacher et al., 1994).

Social skill training facilitates impulse control by encouraging persons

- to stop their ongoing behavior in anger-provoking situations and
- to think about appropriate responses.

Researches have shown good results of behavioral coping and social skills training intervention in anger management among male community volunteers (Rimm et al., 1974) and angry college students (Deffenbacher et al., 1987; Deffenbacher et al., 1994; Deffenbacher et al., 1996).

STRESS INOCULATION TRAINING

Stress inoculation training (SIT) was originally developed to treat anxiety but was adapted for the treatment of angry persons (Meichenbaum and Turk, 1976; Novaco, 1975, 1979).

SIT is a structured treatment program delivered in three phases

- Treatment begins with the cognitive preparation phase in which the angry person learns a new conceptualization of anger that stresses the role of cognition.
- In the skill acquisition and rehearsal phase, angry person receives a combination of cognitive restructuring/self-instructional training, relaxation, and behavioral coping skills.
- Finally, angry persons practice applying the skills they have learned in various contexts, during the application and practice phase.

Researches have shown that SIT interventions are very useful for anger reduction among:

- College students and community volunteers (Novaco, 1975).
- Adult hypertensive patients (Achmon et al., 1989).
- Highly angry college students (Deffenbacher et al., 1990).
- Aggressive parents (Acton and During, 1992).
- Prison inmates (Smith and Backner, 1993).
- Male veterans referred for outpatient anger management (Timmons et al., 1997).

COGNITIVE RELAXATION COPING SKILLS

Cognitive relaxation coping skills (CRCS) was developed by combining cognitive restructuring with a relaxation-based adaptation of anxiety management training by Deffenbacher and his colleagues (1987, 1988).

The primary difference between SIT and CRCS is a reduced emphasis on behavioral coping skills in CRCS and the way in which the treatment is conducted.

- CRCS treatment usually begins with the relaxation component as relaxation can help make cognitive interventions more acceptable (Deffenbacher et al., 1988).
- Once the angry persons are trained in progressive muscle relaxation and several specific relaxation coping skills, then the treatment focuses on cognitive restructuring.

- The angry persons are made to rehearse both relaxation and cognitive coping skills to reduce anger elicited within the therapy session.
- As a client's self-control increases, the anger arousal level is increased, and the therapist's assistance is decreased.

CRCS has shown good results in reducing anger among:

- Highly angry college students (Deffenbacher et al., 1987, 1988, 1990, 1994, 1996),
- Angry drivers (Deffenbacher et al., 2000; Deffenbacher et al., 2000),
- Abusive parents or those identified as 'high risk' to abuse their children (Whitman et al., 1987).

PROVOCATION HIERARCHY WORK

Provocation is simulated (mimicked as if it is a real life situation) in the therapeutic context by imaginal and role-play exposure to anger triggering incidents, anchored in the client's life experiences, as directed by the therapist.

- The provocation incidents are graduated in anger intensity and are arranged as hierarchy exposure, done in conjunction with the teaching of coping skills across sessions (Meichenbaum, 1985).
- The therapist helps the client to arrange a gradation of personally provoking situations, constructing scenes providing sufficient detail to generate a good imaginal image.
- Details about the procedure for individual treatment are given in a therapist manual (Novaco, 2001) and elaborated further in Taylor and Novaco (2005).

RELAXATION COPING SKILLS

Most angry persons have heightened emotional and physiological arousal that most often characterizes the experience of anger. Relaxation based interventions are targeted at the following:

- Angry persons are trained in progressive relaxation and a range of relaxation coping skills, which are then applied for anger reduction within and between sessions.

- As the persons reduce their anger arousal through relaxation, they feel calmer and more in control.
- This helps them to use and access other behavioral skills and more adaptive problem-solving approaches for anger reduction.

The best modes of therapy are the combination of three strategies that have shown good result in studies (Deffenbecher, 2001). These are Relaxation, Cognitive Therapy, and Skill Development.

'Relaxation' is a very effective treatment in managing anger among patients. Clinicians train patients in progressive relaxation until they can quickly use personal cues, such as words, phrases, or images, to relax in an anger-inducing situation.

- People are made to identify what makes them very angry.
- With drivers, for example, a common cause of anger is when people flip them off or go too slow.
- They are made to visualize such a situation intensely for a minute or two and then helped to relax; so the process requires that they first get angry and then relax it away. This is done over and over again.
- By the end of approximately eight sessions, the angry persons learn to relax themselves without a therapist's assistance.

COGNITIVE THERAPY

A psychologist helps patients to see alternative ways of thinking and reacting to anger. This is the most effective technique of anger management.

- A are a lot of ways in which we think when we are angry and they make situations worse.
- Suppose you're driving to work and you get cut off. You think that the driver is an 'idiot'. But you could also think 'Oh that was an accident waiting to happen'.
- If one is an angry parent, one needs to learn parenting skills and if one is an angry driver, he/she needs safe driving skills.

SKILL DEVELOPMENT

Social skills approaches address dysfunctional means of dealing with anger and attempt to provide angry individuals with conflict management skills such as recognizing the impact of their behavior on others, taking time out, and developing listening and feedback skills, assertion, and interpersonal negotiation. As these skills are deployed, anger is reduced as the person communicates more effectively and aborts or reduces cycles of escalating conflict and anger (Deffenbacher et al., 1996).

Relaxation coping skills

- Target both emotional and physiological arousals associated with anger with the intent being to lower the anger arousal.

Cognitive interventions

- Target biases in information processing and cognitive appraisals. They help to identify distorted patterns of thinking, develop more reality-based and less anger-engendering cognitions, and free up problem-solving and coping resources. Dahlen and Deffenbacher (2001).

RATIONAL EMOTIVE BEHAVIOR THERAPY

Rational emotive behavior therapy (REBT) developed by Dr Albert Ellis in 1998 is the most important cognitive behavior therapy. He suggested that anger occurs as a result of one's perceptions and thus can be managed by thinking one's way out of unhealthy anger expression. His approach is designed to help clients become aware of how thoughts and feelings are related.

According to REBT, there are four main classes of cognitive distortions, which are described as 'negative, irrational core beliefs'.

- These distortions are *negative* because holding these beliefs are self-limiting and block further personal development.
- They are *irrational* because they are not based on sufficient evidence to become a hard and fast rule for effective living.
- They are *core* in that they operate at the super-ordinate level of the individual's cognitive structures and thus have a pervasive influence on a large portion of the person's thinking, feelings, and behavior.

Through REBT people can learn a process of reconstruction in which they challenge their old, irrational beliefs, and generate new, potentially more adaptive beliefs.

- As more adaptive beliefs get established, the emotional reactivity of adolescents becomes less, and they are more able to become effective problem solvers, rather than simply reactors to environmental stimuli.
- REBT emphasises on 'what happens to adolescents when they get angry', teaches them that they do not have to be a victim of their circumstances, and help, them to construct alternatives, which become pathways to healthier beliefs, attitudes, and behaviors.
- The REBT model helps adolescents how to replace their maladaptive core beliefs with more adaptive beliefs.

ANGER MANAGEMENT INTERVENTION

There are a variety of anger management interventions for children and adolescents that have been well tried and have become very popular in a variety of settings, e.g., at school, in family, and for residential treatment.

ANGER MANAGEMENT INTERVENTION IN THE SCHOOL CONTEXT

Anger management intervention is very popular in school setting. There are few published research reports on anger management intervention in middle or senior high school settings (Feindler and Scalley, 1998).

One of such program is the 'Think First Program' developed by Feindler and her colleagues. This program combines the elements of anger control and social problem solving specifically oriented toward school-related interpersonal aggression.

- The intervention procedures emphasize the use of prerecorded and in-group videotaping, which helps to demonstrate the use of each anger management skill during an interpersonal conflict.

- This 10-session program has been used extensively in high school settings, and students receiving treatments were found to manifest significantly fewer suspensions and administrative referrals for disruptive behavior than students in the control group (Larson, 1998).

The brain power program (Hudley et al., 1998)

A 12-sesson attribution retraining intervention was implemented for aggressive and non-aggressive boys in four urban public schools.

- Based upon the link between faulty attributions and aggression, this program helps children to recognize accidental causes in peer interactions and to view negative outcomes as a result of accidental and non-hostile cues.
- Once typical hostile attribution bias is reduced, the children display significantly lower levels of aggressive behavior.

KEEPING COOL

A group for eight teenage boys with documented emotional and behavioral difficulties (Dwivedi and Gupta, 2000) was assembled.

- The eight-session program modeled after Feindler and Ecton (1986) was implemented by the school psychologist and a special education teacher.
- Anecdotal feedback indicated that all of the participants became aware of aggressive triggers and feelings.

MULTIPLE BASELINE SINGLE-SUBJECT DESIGN (WHITFIELD, 1999)

An adolescent day treatment program in a public school.

- Eight male students having problems with self-control of disruptive behavior were matched to eight male control subjects.
- The five basic components of the Feindler and Ecton (1986)— self-instruction, self-assessment, self-evaluation, arousal management, and adaptive skill development—were incorporated in 12 one-hour individual sessions.

- All subjects completed self-report measures each week (the Anger Control and Anger Expression subscales of the STAXI and the Self Control Rating Scale) and the staff completed a daily report on aggressive episodes and specific instances of rule violations.
- Results indicated that patterns of improvement on the self-report measures were noted for four treatment subjects while three remained unchanged and one showed a pattern of deterioration.

CHILDREN'S SELF-MANAGEMENT OF ACADEMIC BEHAVIOR

Self-management interventions are helpful for children with aggression and conduct problems.

- It teaches children skills in self-monitoring, self-evaluation, and sometimes self-reinforcement.
- It involves increasing on-task behavior, work-completion behaviors rates, and accuracy of academic work.
- Children develop skills that increase their engagement in learning activities and result in greater learning.
- Children are trained to observe and objectively record their own behavior (self-monitor), compare their behavior to a set of standards (self-evaluation), and administer a reward if they determine they have met the standard (self-reinforcement).

Self-management techniques have produced positive effects on academic behaviors for children with behavioral problems (Levendoski and Cartledge, 2000; Nelson et al., 1991).

FAMILY ANGER MANAGEMENT INTERVENTION

A model of the development of anger in the family and peer contexts suggests the family as the place where emotional socialization takes place (Debaryshe and Fryxell, 1998).

- Family members may function as 'emotional coaches'.
- They provide models for regulation of anger arousal as well as direct instruction for recognizing and interpreting anger experiences.
- In addition to the shaping of a child's behavioral, cognitive, and physiological reactivity to emotional states, a family also provides exposure to interpersonal conflicts and experience in conflict resolution.
- Unresponsive parents or those who suffer from their own emotional deregulation and are less likely to assist their child in the development of healthy emotional control.
- On the other hand, there is a 'difficult temperament' child, who stresses and challenges the unprepared or unskilled parent.
- Additionally, family conflict and maltreatment in the early years influences the development of anger and aggression.
- Various family anger management interventions have been documented.

A Parent Training Approach

It is for abusive parents and parents of aggressive youth who incorporate a number of cognitive strategies contained in anger control training (Stern and Azar, 1998).

- Their cognitive parenting model focuses on the identification of unrealistic expectations and negative attributional biases as well as on poor problem-solving skills, which increase the likelihood of maladaptive and aggressive, parenting response.
- Their parents and families receive skills training in stress and anger management as well as communication and conflict resolution designed to prevent further aggressive parenting.

Role of Anger Management in the Reduction of Parent–Adolescent Conflict (Stern, 1999)

- Parents who were experiencing problematic conflicts at the home were assigned to a conflict management and conflict resolution intervention.
- The obtained results indicated that parents and adolescents involved in angry and coercive conflicts could learn to effectively resolve their issue and communicate more positively.

PARENT FAMILY SKILLS TRAINING

Parent family skills training (PFST) teaches parents and families skills that enhance child, parent, and family functioning (Miller and Prinz, 1990; Taylor and Biglan, 1998).

- PFST is very effective in bringing about change in child, parent, and family functioning when applied to children with anger and aggression problems.
- PEST focuses on important child, parent, parent–child interaction and family target areas e.g.,
    - The first target is reducing children's overt aggression, conduct problems, and noncompliance.
    - The second target is changing problematic parent behaviors such as inadvertent reinforcement of negative child behavior, frequent and ineffective commands, harsh and inconsistent discipline, poor monitoring, and inattentiveness to positive child behavior.
    - The third target is improving the emotional bond between a child and a parent.
    - The fourth target is dealing with the parent's personal problems (e.g., mental health, relational, financial, social, community difficulties) that causes stress for the parent and interfere with optimal parenting.
    - The final target is improving the way family members communicate with one another and solve family problems.

PFST protocols attempt to improve some or all of these target areas simultaneously. Once they are improved, the child will likely exhibit enhanced development in multiple domains of functioning.

Children whose parents participated in PFST do improve, as evidenced by parent and teaching ratings and by direct observation of their behavior (Kazdin, 1997; Taylor and Biglan, 1998).

- Researchers have documented maintenance of intervention gains for 1–3 years, and in some instances, for up to 10–14 years.
- Children below 6 years of age obtained slightly better outcomes with PFST than children who were 6 to 12 years old.

- Researchers have also found that siblings and parents are better adjusted after PFST.

There are several other important therapeutic interventions to controlling anger as discussed below.

HYPNOSIS

Anger can be transformed and eliminated through hypnosis.

- Hypnosis is an effective means to manage, control, and heal anger.
- This anger management system provides: professional guidance, meditation and if needed, even clinical hypnosis.
- This gives the necessary components to gain control over anger and harness it into something that can even be beneficial to the individual and those around him.
- This anger management system is perfect for people who want to gain control of their anger, improve their communication skills, and save their important relationships.

ANGER COPING PROGRAM

Anger coping program is also useful strategy in controlling anger (Lochman et al., 2001). It assists children in the development of skills needed to better understand a peer's perspective and to increase awareness of one's anger signs.

- It involves discussion and role-playing, so that aggressive children will eventually apply and generalize what they have learned to the naturalistic setting.

LEARN MINDFULNESS

Mindfulness is a skill, which enables us to pay attention to the present moment in a non-judgmental way. Learning such a skill may assist us in reacting less to trigger situations.

Kassinove and Tafrate (2002) provided following therapeutic interventions for anger management.

1. Preparing for change:
   a. First of all, clinicians need to start by helping patients increase their motivation and awareness of their anger.
2. Changing:
   b. This stage includes assertiveness training, avoiding, and escaping from anger-invoking situations, and a 'barb exposure technique' that triggers patents' anger and then teaches them to relax.
3. Accepting and adjusting:
   c. At this stage, patients are taught how to reconceptualize their anger triggers, forgive others, and avoid carrying grudges against those who might anger them.
4. Maintaining change:
   d. It's better to conclude treatment with a long-term plan. New triggers might re-ignite anger, so we try to include relapse prevention training.

SPIRITUALITY

Spirituality energizes an individual to desire heightened potential. People who maintain spirituality in their lives report that they live more fully in the present and act more readily from the heart because their minds are free of plans, schemes, inhibitions, and motives.

Additionally, people that claim to have a spiritual connection watch their emotional triggers. When anger or other negative emotions arise meditation can be used to identify the desires and obstacles, to make changes or accept what cannot be changed (Leifer, 1999).

Relationship connectedness, self-transcendence, inner strength, joy, hope, peace, affection, caring, meditation, mindfulness, forgiveness, compassion, etc. are other important characteristics of spirituality that have been proved in treating many psychological problems like stress, depression, and anger.

Vedic philosophy offers a holistic view of exercise, meditation, rest, *mantras*, breathing exercises, and healthy diet (Chopra, 1990).

Simple meditation techniques practiced regularly give a person a feeling of physical and emotional well-being. Sri Sri Ravi Shanker (The Art of Living) and Baba Ramdev (Patnjali University, Haridwar) have offered many such techniques that have been proved in reducing both physiological and psychological distress including anger.

Figure 3.77   Spirituality guru

In Medicine it is said that there is a PILL for every ILL. But there is NO SPECIFIC PILL for anger.

Many practitioners and psychiatrists generally prescribe medication to control episodes of anger but there is no pill specifically designed to address anger. Therefore a layman should not think of a quick treatment for anger related problems.

We have emphasized many tips for self-anger management as well as on the part of family, school, and workplace. Therapeutic interventions discussed in this last section are the only solution for the chronic anger. We hope that by applying these simple anger management tips, a layman would be healthy both physically and psychologically.

SUMMARY

Numerous anger management interventions have been addressed by the researchers and practiced by professionals in school, family, and workplace. Yet every day media is filled with with stories of family conflicts, school bullying, and workplace aggression, which shows that people have not understood that anger is an evil emotion and we need to keep it under control if we want peace and harmony in our life and this world.

Keeping this in mind, we planned the present book for laypersons. People can reduce their everyday anger problems by following the simple steps discussed in this book.

We hope that the readers will be able to control their anger by the simple techniques we have described. This will make our time spent on writing this book worthwhile.

We need to accept that anger management requires training and do not be ashamed to take professional help.

REFERENCES

Achmon, J., Granek, M., Golomb, M., and Hart, J. (1989). 'Behavioral Treatment of Essential Hypertension: A Comparison between Cognitive Therapy and Biofeedback of Heart Rate', *Psychosomatic Medicine*, 51: 152–64.

Acton, R., and During, S. (1992). 'Preliminary Results of Aggression Management Training for Aggressive Parents', *Journal of Interpersonal Violence*, 7: 410–17.

Beck, R., and Fernandez, E. (1998). 'Cognitive-behavioral Therapy in the Treatment of Anger: A Meta-analysis', *Cognitive Therapy and Research*, 22: 63–74.

Bernstein, D. A., and Borkovec, T. D. (1973). *Progressive Relaxation Training: A Manual for the Helping Profession*. Champaign, IL: Research Press.

Catalano, R. F., Loeber, R., and McKinney, K. C. (1999). 'School and Community Interventions to Prevent Serious and Violent Offending', *Juvenile Justice Bulletin*, October, 1–12.

Charney, I. (1972). *Marital Love and Hate*. New York: MacMillan Co.

Chopra, D. (1990). *Perfect Health. The Complete Mind/Body Guide*. New York: Bantam Books.

Dahlen, E. R., and Deffenbacher, J. L. (2001). 'Anger Management', in W. J. Lyddon and J. V. Jones, Jr. (eds.), *Empirically Supported Cognitive Therapies: Current and Future Applications* (pp. 163–81). New York: Springer Publishing Company.

Dahlberg, C. (1998). 'Youth Violence in United States: Major Trends, Risk Factors, and Preventive Approaches', *American Journal of Preventive Medicine*, 14: 259–72.

Debaryshe, B. D., and Fryxell, D. (1998). 'A Developmental Perspective on Anger: Family and Peer Contexts', *Psychology in the Schools*, 35: 205–16.

Deffenbacher, J. L. (1988). 'Cognitive-relaxation and Social Skills Treatments of Anger: A Year Later', *Journal of Counseling Psychology*, 35: 234–36.

———. (1994). 'Anger Reduction: Issues, Assessment, and Intervention Strategies', in A. W. Siegman and T. W. Smith (eds.), *Anger, Hostility, and the Heart* (pp. 239–69). Hillsdale, New Jersey: Erlbaum.

———. (1995). Ideal Treatment Package for Adults with Anger Disorders, in H. Kassinove (ed.), *Anger Disorders: Definition, Diagnosis and Treatment* (pp. 151–72). Philadelphia, Pennsylvania: Taylor and Francis.

———. (1996). 'Cognitive-behavioral Approaches to Anger Reduction', in K. S. Dobson and K. D. Craig (eds.), *Advances in Cognitive-behavioral Therapy* (pp. 31–62). Thousand Oaks, California: Sage.

Deffenbacher, J. L., Eugene, Oetting R., Raymond A., and DiGiuseppe, R. A. (2002). 'Principles of Empirically Supported Interventions Applied to Anger Management', *The Counseling Psychologist*, 30: 262.

Deffenbacher, J. L., Filetti, L. B., Lynch, R. S., and Dahlen, E. R. (2000, August). *Interventions for the Reduction of Driving Anger*, paper presented at the 108th Annual Convention of the American Psychological Association, Washington, D.C.

Deffenbacher, J. L., Huff, M.E., Lynch, R. S., Getting, E. R., and Salvatore, N. F. (2000). 'Characteristics and Treatment of High-anger Drivers', *Journal of Counseling Psychology*, 47: 5–17.

Deffenbacher, J. L., McNamara, K., Stark, R. S., and Sabadell, P. M. (1990). 'A Combination of Cognitive, Relaxation, and Behavioral Coping Skills in the Reduction of General Anger', *Journal of College Student Development*, 31: 351–58.

Deffenbacher, J. L., Oetting, E. R., Thwaites, G. A., Lynch, R. S., Baker, D. A., and Stark, P. S. (1996). 'State-trait Anger Theory and the Utility of the Trait Anger Scale', *Journal of Counseling Psychology*, 43: 131–48.

Deffenbacher, J. L., Story, D. A., Stark, R. S., Hogg, J. A., and Brandon, A. D. (1987). 'Cognitive-relaxation and Social Skills Interventions in the Treatment of General Anger', *Journal of Counseling Psychology*, 34: 171–76.

Deffenbacher, J. L., Story, D. A., Brandon, A. D., Hogg, J. A., and Hazaleus, S. L. (1988). 'Cognitive and Cognitive-relaxation Treatments of Anger', *Cognitive Therapy and Research*, 12: 167–84.

Deffenbacher, J. L., Thwaites, G. A., Wallace, T. L., and Oetting, E. R. (1994). 'Social Skills and Cognitive-relaxation Approaches to General Anger Reduction', *Journal of Counseling Psychology*, 41: 386–96.

Dwivedi, K., and Gupta, A. (2000). '"Keeping Cool" Anger Management through Group Work', *Support for Learning*, 15(2): 76–81

Ellis, A. (1998). How Rational Emotive Behavior Therapy Belongs in the Constructive Camp, in M.F. Hoyt (ed.), *The Handbook of Constructivist Therapies*. San Francisco: Jossey-Bass, pp. 83–99.

Enright, R. D. (2002). *Forgiveness is a Choice: A Step-by-step Process for Resolving Anger and Restoring Hope*. Washington, D.C.: American Psychological Association.

Everson SA, Kaplan GA, Goldberg DE, Lakka TA, Sivenius J, and Salonen JT. (1999). 'Anger Expression and Incident Stroke. Prospective Evidence from the Kuopio Ischemic', Heart Disease Study. *Stroke*, 30: 523–28.

Feindler, E. L., and Ecton, R. B. (1986). *Adolescent Anger Control: Cognitive-behavioral Techniques*. New York: Pergamon Press.

Feindler, E. L., and Scalley, M. (1998). Group Anger Management Approaches to Violence Prevention, in K. Stoiber and T. R. Ollendick (eds.), *Handbook of Group Intervention for Children and Families*, (pp. 100–119) Needham Heights, MA: Allyn and Bacon.

Franz, C. E, McClelland, D. C., and Weinberger, J. (1991). 'Childhood Antecedents of Conventional Social Accomplishment in Midlife Adults: A 36-year Prospective Study', *Journal of Personality and Social Psychology*, 60: 586–95.

Futterman, L. G., and Lemberg, L. (2002). 'Anger and Acute Coronary Events', *American Journal of Critical Care*, 11: 574–76

Gibson, D. E., and Barsade, S. G. (1999, August). 'The Experience of Anger at Work: Lessons from the Chronically Angry', in R. R. Callister (Chair), *Anger in Organizations: Its Causes and Consequences*. Symposium Presented at the Annual Meeting of the Academy of Management Conference, Chicago.

Goldstein, J. (1999). 'The Attractions of Violent Entertainment', *Media Psychology*, 1: 271–82.

Goldstein, A. P., Harootunian, B., and Conotey, J. C. (1999). *Student Aggression: Prevention, Management and Replacement Training*. New York: Guilford Press.

Hartig, T., Evans, G. W., Jamner, L. J., Davis, D. S., and Gärling, T. (2003) 'Tracking Restoration in Natural and Urban Field Settings', *Journal of Environmental Psychology*, 23: 109–23.

Hazaleus, S. L., and Deffenbacher, J. L. (1986). 'Relaxation and Cognitive Treatments of Anger', *Journal of Consulting and Clinical Psychology*, 54: 222–26.

Holmes, J. (1990). 'Apologies in New Zealand English', *Lang. Soc.* 19: 155–99.

Hudley, C. A., Britsch, B., Wakefield, W. D., Smith, T., Demorat, M., and Cho, S. (1998). 'An Attribution Retraining Program to Reduce Aggression in Elementary School Students', *Psychology in the School*, 35: 271–82.

Kassinove, H., and Tafrate, R. C. (2002). *Anger Management: The Complete Practitioner's Guidebook for the Treatment of Anger*. Atascadero, CA: Impact Publishers.

Kaufer, S., and Mattman, J. (2004). *Workplace Violence: An Employer's Guide*. Online at http://www.workplaceviolence.com/articles/employers_guide.htm (downloaded in January 2007).

Kaufman, P., Chen, X., and Choy, S. P. (2001). *Indicators of School Crime and Safety*. Publication No. NCES 2002-113/NCJ-190075. Washington, DC: U.S. Departments of Education and Justice.

Kazdin, A. (1997). 'Parent Management Training: Evidence, Outcomes, and Issues', *Journal of the American Academy of Child and Adolescent Psychiatry*, 36: 1349–58.

Larson, J. D. (1998). 'Managing Student Aggression in High School: Implications for Practice', *Psychology in School*, 35(3): 283–95.

Leifer, R. (1999). 'Buddhist Conceptualization and Treatment of Anger', *Journal of Clinical Psychology*, 55(3): 339–51.

Levendoski, L. S., and Cartledge, G. (2000). 'Self-monitoring for Elementary School Children with Serious Emotional Disturbances: Classroom Applications for Increased Academic Responding', *Behavioral Disorders*, 25: 211–24.

Mace, D., and Mace, V. (1974). *We Can Have Better Marriages if We Really Want Them*. Nashville, Tenn: Abingdon Press.

Meichenbaum, D. (1985). *Stress Inoculation Training*. Elmsford, NY: Pergamon Press.

Meichenbaum, D., and Turk, D. C. (1976). 'The Cognitive Behavioral Management of Anxiety, Anger and Pain', in P. Davidson (ed.), *The Behavioral Management of Anxiety, Depression and Pain*. New York: Brunner/Mazel.

Miller, G. E., and Prinz, R. J. (1990). 'Enhancement of Social Learning Family Interventions for Child Conduct Disorder', *Psychological Bulletin*, 108: 291–307.

Miller, P., and Sperry, L. (1987). 'The Socialization of Anger and Aggression', *Merrill-Palmer Quarterly*, 33(1): 1–31.

Moon, J. R., and Eisler, R. M. (1983). 'Anger Control: An Experimental Comparison of Three Behavioral Treatments', *Behavior Therapy*, 14: 493–505.

Moore, M., and Dahlen, E. R. (2008). 'Forgiveness and Consideration of Future Consequences in Aggressive Driving', *Accident Analysis and Prevention*, 40: 1661–66.

Nelson, J. R., Smith, D. J., Young, K. R., and Dodd, J. M. (1991). A Review of Self-management Outcome Research Conducted with Students who Exhibit Behavioral Disorders. *Behavioral Disorders*, 16: 169–79.

Novaco, R. (1975). *Anger Control: The Development and Evaluation of an Experimental Treatment*. Lexington, MA: Lexington Books.

———. (1979). 'Cognitive Regulation of Anger and Stress', in P. Kendall and S. Hollon (eds.), *Cognitive-behavioral Interventions: Theory, Research, and Procedures* (pp. 241–85). New York: Academic Press.

Ohbuchi, K., Kameda, M., and Agarie, N. (1989). 'Apology as Aggression Control: Its Role in Mediating Appraisal of and Response to Harm', *Journal of Personality and Social Psychology*, 56: 219–27.

Rimm, D. C., Hill, G. A., Brown, N. H., and Stuart, J. E. (1974). 'Group-assertive Training in Treatment of Expression of Inappropriate Anger', *Psychological Reports*, 34: 794–98.

Stern, S. B., and Azar, S. T. (1998), 'Integrating Cognitive Strategies into Behavioral Treatment of Abusive Parents and Families with Aggressive Adolescents', *Clinical Child Psychology and Psychiatry*, 3: 387–403.

Stern, S. B. (1999). 'Anger Management in Parent-Adolescent Conflict', *American Journal of Family Therapy*, 27(2): 181–93.

Tafrate, R. C., and Kassinove, H. (1998). 'Anger Control among Adult Males: Barb Exposure with Rational, Typical, and Irrelevant Self-statements', *Journal of Cognitive Psychotherapy*, 12: 187–212.

Tavris, C. (1989). *Anger: The Misunderstood Emotion*. New York: Simon and Schuster.

Taylor and Biglan (1998). 'Behavioural Family Interventions for Improving Child Rearing: A Review for Clinicians and Policy Makers', *Clinical Child and Family Psychology Review*, 1: 41–60.

Thomas, S., Groer, M., Davis, M., Droppleman, P., Mozingo, J., and Pierce, M. (2000). Anger and Cancer: An Analysis of the Linkages. *Cancer Nursing*, 23: 344–49.

Timmons, P., Oehlert, M., Sumerall, S., Timmons, C., and Borgers, S. (1997). 'Stress Inoculation Training for Maladaptive Anger: Comparison of Group Counseling versus Computer Guidance', *Computers in Human Behavior*, 13: 51–64.

Whitfield, G. (1999). 'Validating School Social Work: An Evaluation of a Cognitive-behavioral Approach to Reduce School Violence', *Research on Social Work Practice*, 9: 399–426.

Whitman, T. L., Borkowski, J. G., Schellenbach, C. J., and Nath, P. S. (1987). 'Predicting and Understanding Developmental Delay of Children of Adolescent Mothers: A Multi-dimensional Approach', *American Journal of Mental Deficiency*, 92: 40–56.

Appendix: Definitions of Anger

DIFFERENT PHILOSOPHERS AND PSYCHOLOGISTS HAVE DEFINED ANGER DIFFERENTLY

1. *Plato* viewed anger as basically an animal 'passion,' but one in proximity to reason. He arrived at this by dividing the psyche into three parts:

    a. The animal part, filled with irrational passions, or emotions, reside in the trunk of the body.
    b. The immortal, rational part, reside in the head.
    c. A third part, reserved just for anger, reside in and around the chest and neck, and belong both to passions and to reason.

    He viewed anger as a mixed blessing, sometimes good, when rightly provoked, but often a great danger to the state if it caused the individual irrationally to defy the state's authority.

2. *Aristotle* on the other hand, believed that anger was based on judgment, hence, was closely aligned with reason. He held that anger was a natural response to painful situations, and that it involved both the body and the soul.

    Anger was valuable, according to him, and a virtuous person was one who could *'feel anger at the right time, toward the right people, for the right motive'* (Aristotle, 1991).

3. *St. Augustine* defined anger as judgment by which punishment is inflicted on sin.

4. *Anderson* (1978) said that anger may be a defense to avoid painful feelings; it may be associated with failure, low self-esteem, and feelings of isolation; or it may be related to anxiety about situations over which the child has no control.

5. *Spielberger* (1985) has defined anger as an emotional state that varies in intensity from mild irritation to intense fury and rage. He felt anger can be expressed in a variety of ways and this is assessed with State-Trait Anger Expression Inventory (STAXI-2), Spielberger, 1999.

Spielberger's famous scale, 'The State-Trait Anger Expression Inventory', has distinguished between the following:

   a. State-anger: situation specific and not stable.
   b. Trait-anger: stable personality trait that leads to angry reactions.
   c. Anger-in: anger withheld and suppressed. This is a characteristic of individuals who have anxiety and depression.
   d. Anger-out: anger expressed openly physically, verbally or toward the source of irritation.
   e. Anger-control/out: controlling angry feelings by preventing the expression of anger toward other persons or objects.
   f. Anger-control/in: controlling suppressed angry feelings by calming down or cooling off.

6. *Shaver* et al., (1987) say that anger often involves a wide variety of feelings, labeled as irritation, annoyance, disgust, resentment, and fury.

7. *Luhn* (1992) says that anger is made up of different reactions that cause us to be irritated, annoyed, furious, frustrated, enraged, and even hurt. Our response to anger involves our body, our behavior, and our thought process. He argues that it is not the event that causes us to feel angry, but it is how we view the event and provocations that cause us to respond in a specific way.

8. *Deffenbacher* et al., in 1996 said that anger is a common and universally experienced emotion, which occurs on a continuum from mild annoyance to rage or fury. In 2002, Deffenbacher et al. stated that anger is a complex emotion and occurs as a result of an interaction between one or more eliciting events, the individual's pre-anger state, appraisals of the eliciting events, and available coping resources.

9. *Chicago Bible Students* (1996) observed that anger is a strong emotion that expresses displeasure or dislike and can be either constructive or destructive.

10. *Barrett* (1997) described it as the emotion that is the fight for life. It is an important aspect that humans need to survive and live healthy.

11. *Humphrey* (1997) described it as 'primal emotions' or an emotion that is innately rooted as a means of survival.

12. *Evans & Yazdpour* (1997) gave the most important definition of anger i.e., it is a temporary emotional state that is caused by frustration.

13. *Warren* (1990) stated, 'Anger is a physical state of readiness. When we are angry, we are prepared to act' (p. 77).

14. *Marion* (1997) described anger as having three components: the emotional state; the expression; and the understanding of anger, or the interpreting and evaluating.

15. *Capozzoli and McVey* (2000) stated anger is 'A feeling of indignation and hostility that involves complex emotions and depends on how we evaluate events and/or situations'.

16. *Novaco* (2000) stated anger is a negatively toned (unpleasant) emotion and an internal occurrence, which is subjectively experienced as a highly aroused, agitated, and antagonistic state of mind.

Novaco in 1975 had defined anger as having four distinct components: physiological, affective, behavioural, and cognitive.

- The affective component of anger relates to the strength of emotional responses toward anger-provoking situations.
- The behavioural component refers to coping mechanisms, which may be positive or destructive, that people use to express anger.
- The cognitive component reflects the types of negative beliefs, or hostility that people have about the world, and in particular, refers to the negative attributions they hold toward others or places.

17. *Murphy and Oberlin* (2001) stated that anger is 'A powerful response, triggered by another negative emotion that results in an attack of variable intensity that is not always appropriate.' According to them anger is not a pure emotion. There is a broad range of negative emotions that trigger anger—pain, frustration, oneliness, boredom, fear, rejection, jealousy, disappointment, embarrassment, depression, and humiliation, to name just a few'.

18. *Sisco* (1991) stated, 'Sometimes other emotions such as fear, hurt, guilt, shame, sadness, jealousy, frustration, loneliness, even joy, will trigger anger in us. Then anger can become a way of covering up or defending ourselves from these other emotions.'

19. *Warren* (1990) stated that anger places an individual in a state of readiness therefore, one should use that energy immediately so that your body can relax and get back effectively to baseline. If you maintain the state of anger for too long, it may result in considerable physical damage.

20. *Horn and Towl* (1997) stated that anger can occur when a person feels powerless or threatened.

21. In the *American Heritage College Dictionary,* (1993) anger is defined as 'a strong feeling of displeasure or hostility'.

REFERENCES

The American Heritage College Dictionary (3rd ed.). (1993). Boston, MA: Houghton Mifflin Company.

Anderson, L S. (1978). The Aggressive Child. *Pediatric Development and Behavior, 1.* Retrieved March 10, 2002, online at http://www.dbpeds.org/articles/article.cfm (downloaded in December 2007).

Aristotle (1991). *The Nichomachean Ethics.* Oxford, UK: Oxford University Press.

Barrett, B. (1997). *Staff Writings: Anger-the Fight for Life.* PCEC: Anger-The Fight for Life.

Capozzoli, T. K., and McVey, R. S. (2000). *Kids Killing Kids: Managing Violence and Gangs in Schools.* Boca Raton, FL: St. Lucie Press.

Chicago Bible Students test pages (May 20, 1996). *Anger and Love.* Online at webmaster@ chicagobible.org (downloaded in January 2007).

Deffenbacher, J. L., Oetting, E. R., Thwaites, G. R., Lynch, R. S., Baker, D. A., Thaker, S., and Eisworth-Cox, L. (1996). State-trait Anger Theory and the Utility of the Trait Anger Scale. *Journal of Counseling Psychology,* 43(2): 131–48.

Horn, R., and Towl, G. (1997). Anger Management for Women Prisoners. *Issues in Criminological and Legal Psychology,* 29: 57–62.

Humphrey, C. (Fall 1997). *Anger Management: An Interview with Mark too Good.* Father Times, 6. on-line: F.R.C. Home Page/Father Times/F.R.C. Programs.

Luhn, R. R. (1992). *Managing Anger: Methods for a Happier and Healthier Life.* United States of America: Crisp Publications, Inc.

Marion, M. (1997). Helping Young Children Deal with Anger. (Report No. EDO-PS-97- 24). Champaign, IL: *Clearinghouse on Elementary and Early Childhood Education.* (ERIC Document Reproduction Service No. ED414077).

Murphy, T., and Oberlin, L. H. (2001). *The Angry Child: Regaining Control When Your Child is Out of Control.* New York, NY: Clarkson Potter/Publisher.

Novaco, R. W. (1975). *Anger Control: The Development and Evaluation of an Experimental Treatment.* Lexington, MA: Academic Press.

Novaco, R. W. (2000). 'Anger', in A. E. Kazdin (ed.), *Encyclopaedia of Psychology* (pp. 170–74). Washington, DC: American Psychological Association and Oxford University Press.

Shaver, P., Schwartz, J., Kirson, D., and O'Connor, C. (1987). 'Emotion Knowledge: Further Exploration of a Prototype Approach', *Journal of Personality and Social Psychology*, 52: 1061–86.

Spielberger, C. D. (1985). 'Anxiety, Cognition and Affect. A State-trait Perspective', in A. H. Tuma and J. D. Maser (eds.), *Anxiety and Anxiety Disorders* (pp. 109–30). Hillsdale, NJ: Lawrence Erlbaum.

———. (1999). *State-Trait Anger Expression-2. Professional Manual.* Lutz, FL: Psychological Assessment Resources.

Warren, N. C. (1990). *Make Anger Your Ally: Harnessing One of Your Most Powerful Emotions.* Brentwood, TN: Wolgemuth & Hyatt, Inc.

Index

About the Authors

Swati Y. Bhave, Visiting Consultant, Indraprastha Apollo Hospital, New Delhi, is an internationally known pediatrician and adolescent specialist. She is Executive Director of an NGO—Association of Adolescent and Child Care in India (AACCI). She has been the President of Indian Academy of Pediatrics (IAP) in 2000 and presently holds the post of coordinator in the International Pediatric Association (IPA). She is also a member of the Technical Steering Committee (TSC) of the child and adolescent section of WHO, Geneva. She is a former Professor of Pediatrics in BJ Medical College, Pune and Associate Professor in Grant Medical College, Mumbai. She has also worked as a Senior Consultant and PG teacher at the Bombay Hospital Institute of Medical Sciences. She has many medical books to her credit specially in adolescent health and her current interest is adolescent mental health. She has also written books for the layman and participated in many shows on TV and given radio talks. She was Editor of the *Asian Journal of Pediatric Practice* from 1994–2008.

Sunil Saini is doing research work in the Department of Applied Psychology, GJUS&T, Hisar, Haryana, and has a lot of research experience on anger and anger related problems. He has published about 40 research papers in national and international journals and has edited a book with Dr Swati Bhave. He is currently Associate Executive Editor of the journal *Indian Psychologist*.